KNOWING AND LIVING YOUR ORTHODOX CHRISTIAN FAITH
A GUIDE TO FAITH AND WORSHIP

A. S. Bogeatzes

WESTBOW
PRESS

A DIVISION OF THOMAS NELSON

WestBow Press books may be ordered through booksellers or by contacting:

WestBow Press
A Division of Thomas Nelson
1663 Liberty Drive
Bloomington, IN 47403
www.westbowpress.com
1-(866) 928-1240

Because of the dynamic nature of the Internet, any Web addresses or links contained in this book may have changed since publication and may no longer be valid. The views expressed in this work are solely those of the author and do not necessarily reflect the views of the publisher, and the publisher hereby disclaims any responsibility for them.

ISBN: 978-1-4497-0434-6 (sc)
ISBN: 978-1-4497-0476-6 (e)

Library of Congress Control Number: 2010934055

Printed in the United States of America

WestBow Press rev. date: 11/11/2010

In loving memory of my beloved wife, Elizabeth, who led an exemplary life and was such a magnificent wife, mother, grandmother, and friend.
May Her Memory Be Eternal!

CONTENTS

Introduction
MY STRUGGLE TO LEARN MY ORTHODOX FAITH

"Mama, what's he saying?" I was referring to the priest who stood at the altar proclaiming a message in biblical Greek that my English-native ears could not understand. Each foreign word resounded against the walls of our early 1900s building.

At seven years old, I was full of questions, but that particular Sunday after church services, my mother (a native of Greece) could not give me answers. "I didn't understand most of it because it was in *Archaia Ellinika*, ancient biblical Greek," she said.

But if she was from Greece and didn't understand it, how was I supposed to? For years after that experience, I was mystified in trying to understand the Liturgy and the Orthodox Church. My thirst for knowledge would continue to influence much of my life.

In those days, few communities had a Sunday school, although our community had a catechism class (catichico scholio) one day a week as part of Greek school. It was difficult to get a good understanding of what was discussed during the catechism classes, as the discussions were in Modern Greek. The liturgical services, on the other hand, were completely in biblical Greek while the sermons applied Modern Greek. With two different languages to translate and decipher, I began to question if I would ever be able to totally comprehend our Orthodox faith.

When I was sixteen years old and had learned how to drive, I decided to attend a Holy Week service one evening by myself. As I sat there listening to ramblings that my mind could not understand,

I wondered why I was sitting there enduring a service from which I had little to gain. Suddenly, toward the end of the service, I felt a strange and warm feeling come over me, as if someone was trying to tell me something. I wasn't sure how to interpret this feeling, so when the offering tray was passed around, I took all the money from my wallet—a crumpled $10 bill, which was about two weeks' pay for me at that time—and put it in the tray. Even though I felt that I had given money for the Lord, it did not seem to satisfy the vacant feeling inside me.

The fulfillment was yet to come. The following weekend, my church held a Resurrection midnight liturgical service, and I felt compelled to go. Sitting on the wooden pew throughout the candle-lit service, again with very little understanding (in those days, there were no books of translation available for any of the services), once again a sudden warm and deep feeling fell upon me, as if someone was trying to tell me that there was something there that was greater than any lack of understanding I might have. A voice—only audible to my mind—seemed as if to tell me that I should keep trying to learn about my faith and identify myself with the Word of God. This momentous revelation has remained with me at all times throughout my lifetime.

A couple of years later, while in high school, I learned that several other Orthodox churches in our western Pennsylvania area (Serbian, Russian, Ukrainian, and several others) were beginning to use English in part of their services so that the people could begin to gain some understanding of the Liturgy. I had some Serbian friends and went with them to a service one Sunday at their church, and for the first time I began to get some meaning from the Liturgy. I was truly astonished and couldn't understand why the Greek Orthodox churches in our area never even considered using English in at least part of the services up to that time.

Years slipped by, and yet many questions remained unanswered. I grappled with an understanding of what my faith was all about, and my hunger for understanding grew.

After I graduated from college, the new priests in many of the churches in the area were coming out of Holy Cross Seminary and saw a need to educate the people about our Orthodox faith and worship. They even began to give their sermons in both Greek and English. In addition, the Archdiocese instituted the first nationwide young adult group (Greek Orthodox Young Adults [GOYA]; ages 18–31). Not only were we able to experience a great deal of fellowship with Orthodox Christians of our age, but we also could attend educational seminars and workshops in our local chapters and at the district and national conferences. The wave hit, and I was sure to ride in on it.

Young priests began writing books that were educating readers about our Church, all in English, making information more accessible. However, there was one detail I simply could not get over. The Liturgy was still totally in biblical Greek. Even though a few priests made attempts to start in the direction of using some English, the hierarchy in this country prevented their efforts.

The American Greek Orthodox Church at last began to progress somewhat when His Eminence, Archbishop Iakovos, was appointed in 1959. Coincidentally, I was elected to the National Council of GOYA at that time, and shortly after His Eminence was appointed, he was in attendance at our first meeting of the year at the Archdiocese in New York. Following our regular meeting, His Eminence gave a stirring account of how he was going to improve the Greek Orthodox communities in America. His last remark set the tone of his future work: "his ultimate goal was to form one Orthodox Church in America from all the various ethnic Orthodox churches." Those of us at the meeting were truly thrilled and optimistic to hear this.

One year into his leadership, in 1960, his Eminence organized SCOBA (Standing Council of Orthodox Bishops in America), which consists of the leading bishops of each ethnic Orthodox canonical jurisdiction. The organization acts as a clearinghouse to focus the efforts of the Orthodox Church at large on common concerns. At least the voices of the people would be heard.

During his tenure as supreme leader of the Greek Orthodox Church of the Americas, his Eminence Archbishop Iakovos and the other hierarchy under his authority did an extraordinary job and made a great deal of progress of strengthening each community. In addition, more and more of the Greek Orthodox communities began to incorporate English into their liturgical services. An English translation of the Liturgy also began to appear in the church pews in many of the communities. The roles of the priest and the parish council were clearly defined so that the spiritual, administrative, and organizational aspects in each community could be properly coordinated. Through Archbishop Iakovos's efforts, each community became stabilized as they embraced the foundation of the Greek Orthodox Church in America.

However, his Eminence's efforts to establish one Ethnic Orthodox Church in America were subdued by the Patriarch of Constantinople.

Over time, the communities became a source where each member can lay the groundwork for our Orthodox Christian faith and establish a true rapport with one another and a relationship with our Lord. Archbishop Iakovos, with his outstanding achievements in leading the Greek Orthodox Church in America, established sound and effective church communities, so that future steps can be taken toward active parishioner commitment as they learn about their Orthodox faith and participate faithfully each and every Sunday in the Divine Liturgy.

I personally made little progress at first in achieving a thorough understanding of the faith and worship of the Orthodox Church, especially in the Divine Liturgy. While the interest in the heritage and traditions of my faith were important to me, my advancement was essentially stagnant. After reading numerous books, attending countless seminars and workshops, and studying tapes and videos, I still had so many questions.

Then a breakthrough came for me in 1979 when I decided to attend the Liturgy at Holy Trinity Greek Orthodox Church, Westfield, NJ, upon the urging of several members there. I was amazed! This was the first Liturgy I had attended in which most of it was performed in a language I could completely understand. I was impressed with how powerful it was, not only because the language barrier had crumbled but also because of the way that the parish priest, Father Alexander Leondis, had structured it. I had never before seen a Liturgy that included several prayers repeated together in English by the congregation. There were also books of translation nestled in all the pews. I could not get over the great feeling of participation I got in being able to completely partake in and follow nearly every word of the service.

After my wife and I attended the Liturgy the following Sunday, we immediately joined Holy Trinity. The Divine Liturgy at Westfield, NJ, as established by Father Alexander Leondis, is truly a model demonstrating to other communities how to utilize the service to increase congregational participation in the Liturgy.

Shortly after achieving devotion with our new church home, I became active in the Sunday school. When I was asked to become director, one of my major objectives was to expand the curriculum of the Sunday school. In expanding the upper grades (7–12), we had to develop our own curriculum because the Archdiocese Religious Education Department had only developed a curriculum for the lower grades at that time. I opened communications with the director of the Archdiocese Religious Education Department, Mr. Ernest Villas, about expanding the curriculum. To my surprise, he agreed that the department should proceed in expanding the Sunday school curriculum, and my objective was set.

Needless to say, even though Mr. Villas agreed that effort should be made in this area, progress was slow. I did not allow this stumbling block to slow me down. Holy Trinity continued to develop much of the curriculum on its own. When eventually a National Curriculum Committee formed, the Archdiocese reiterated its recommendation for curriculum for both lower and part of the upper grades, and Holy Trinity Sunday School or Religious Education School, as it is known today, held the honor of contributing significantly in integrating various aspects of our Orthodox faith that I had learned and compiled over the years.

My spiritual ups and downs testify to the many years and varied experiences that I had to go through so that I could be blessed by our Lord to be able to gain the understanding of our Orthodox faith and worship. And I still have a long way to go! My aspiration is that it doesn't take too many more years to acquire a worthy and acceptable understanding of our beloved faith, as much as my ability permits.

Through what I have witnessed, I've come to understand the importance of our hierarchy and clergy in America to make an earnest effort to formulate and establish a means for the members of the Greek Orthodox Church communities to gain an in-depth understanding of the Orthodox faith and worship. Worshipers should be made aware of the continuity and connection of our Orthodox Church with our Lord and Savior and His disciples and apostles. If clear wisdom can be achieved in the early stages of a believer's life, it opens up opportunity for their later years to be spent further cherishing and treasuring our Lord.

It should not have to take a lifetime of effort to gain understanding of our Church: *That the Church is the Body of Christ—with Him at the Head; that the Orthodox Church has maintained the teachings, beliefs, doctrines, and traditions of Jesus Christ as established by His disciples and apostles; that the Liturgy has been unchanged for more than 1,500 years, and thus represents the original worship services as established by the disciples, apostles, and early Church Fathers.*

History shows that the Orthodox Church has greater continuity with the original established Church than any other Christian denomination today. It is essential that all Orthodox Christians truly embrace this in order to proceed with a better understanding of the faith, worship, and beliefs. All Orthodox Christians should acquire this insight of our Orthodox faith and wholly participate in the Liturgy. They should also say their prayers daily, read the Bible regularly, and faithfully attend services.

I am encouraged by the direction that many of our priests are taking in establishing a Liturgy that utilizes less biblical Greek—which often consists of shorter commentaries—in favor of preferred English.

This allows for fewer distractions from the change of language, and thus more continuity in the liturgical service. This definitely improves *the harmony of the priest and the believers in the Divine Liturgy.* Religious education classes, coupled with Bible classes, are also frequently held in many communities to educate the members in our Orthodox faith and worship.

Christ, Himself, in His final instructions to His apostles said, *"Go therefore and make disciples of all nations, baptizing them in the name of the Father, and of the Son, and of the Holy Spirit. Teaching them to learn all whatsoever I have instructed and commanded you."* (Matthew 28:19). In a similar manner, the hierarchy and leaders of the Orthodox Church, along with those of other Christian faiths, are also to carry out Christ's instructions, as did the apostles, not only to the members of their own churches but also to all nations and people of the world.

Throughout the years, I prepared various notes and writings when I studied a Church topic in detail. Much like that warm and wonderful feeling I had in church on the day when I was sixteen years old, I felt inspired to organize and compile the various topics into one comprehensive book. After all, if there had been a resource like that available during my youth, I could have embarked on my spiritual journey much sooner in life. Oddly, the preparation of this document did not come as a laborious or wearisome effort on my part. Anytime I was doing other things like attending church, exercising, driving, reading, or even watching my favorite sports and dramas on TV, my thoughts would always return to my writings. I would say the Jesus Prayer, and some new ideas or changes in the existing write-up would filter into my mind. I would immediately take notes, and as soon as I could, I'd run to my computer and incorporate my thoughts into the manuscript. All in all, for me it was a privilege and a mark of distinction to have the desire and inspiration to prepare this book. Knowing that my work is dedicated to the memory of my beloved and magnificent wife, Elizabeth, was also a great motivation to me. I sincerely hope that this resource will be useful to other Orthodox Christians, giving them an adequate awakening to the wisdom of their Church so that they can completely embrace their Orthodox faith. There also may be instances where various clergy can also make use of these writings to better educate their believers in the doctrines, beliefs, holy traditions, and worship of our beloved Orthodox Christian faith.

Chapter 1

THE ORTHODOX CHRISTIAN CHURCH:
THE TRUE PATH TO JESUS

Overcoming Our Struggle

Orthodox, Protestant, Catholic, Nondenominational. With so many denominations of Christianity, our faiths can easily muddle the fine lines that differentiate the various belief systems. What does being an Orthodox Christian mean in today's world?

I struggled with this question during my childhood and well into my adulthood. Like me, many Orthodox Christians stumble throughout our lives, trying to establish our Christian beliefs and principles in order to live the life that Christ directs us to live. If we continue to learn about our faith and constantly commit ourselves to Jesus, we may get to a point where we at least become somewhat content and at peace in this struggle. However, it is a continual process, for trying to achieve the ultimate goal of *theosis,* or becoming Christ-like, is a lifelong battle; after all, we are only human and not perfect. Only Christ can claim perfection.

Going Out on Our Own

Doubts and questions often arise the first time we leave our parents' home and venture out on our own, especially those who go off to college, where they are exposed to many lifestyles and a wide range of new philosophies and ideas. The different values and viewpoints that you are exposed to when you first step into the world may have an adverse impact on your faith. There are many out there who want to challenge your thinking and feelings on what you learned about Orthodox Christianity while you were growing up.

For some of us, it may take time and a renewed effort to overcome any unfavorable attitudes we develop during these transitional years. You may have stopped attending church services regularly or forgone reading the Holy Bible faithfully during this period. But eventually, you will once again face those deep theological questions rooted in your spirit. When you return to your Christian beliefs and traditions, you still may be challenged to find all the answers that you are seeking to attain total and complete fulfillment in your Orthodox faith.

I went through the period of questions and uncertainties during my college days as an engineering student and for some time thereafter. The instructors in our science and engineering classes tried to teach us that scientific theories and formulas were absolute and separate from any other power or influence. According to "pure science," the structure of the atoms or the hypotheses and formulas for forces, matter, and energy were a total explanation of matter and nature, and of the universe. There were no further clarifications needed, nor was there a presence of any other power. When one would ask where the atoms or forces came from or who caused such a natural order and balance in our planet earth, our universe, or the human body, no explanations would be given. From science's perspective, God could not be the intelligent designer.

When I first decided to pursue engineering, I read a book by Albert Einstein, a man thought to be one of the greatest thinkers in the known history of civilization. Dr. Einstein was not only an outstanding scientist and great teacher at Princeton but also an exceptional author. He could explain his numerous complex theories, such as his atomic theory and theory of relativity, in language that the common person could grasp. I read this book years ago and don't recall many of the details, but there was one point I do remember vividly, and that was his closing sentence: "The closer one comes to reality about life and nature, the more one realizes that there is some greater power behind all this that we will never completely comprehend." Fortunately, this sentence stayed with me and influenced me greatly during this period of skepticism. I was impressed with his declaration, even though some considered Dr. Einstein an agnostic or an atheist. It was a great inspiration to me in my eventual total acceptance of the absolute power of an infinite God in all things.

Finding the Answers

When we face questions about our faith and in our Lord Jesus Christ, where do we turn to find answers? If you truly want to understand something, you have to get a grasp on how it got started and evolved. Knowing the original helps us know the end result. For example, we are taught extensively in our history classes about how the Founding Fathers established the government, uniting the original colonies, and how they evolved into the great and magnificent nation we are fortunate to be a part of today—the United States of America. This knowledge enables us to be more responsible citizens. Similarly, we can strengthen and build our Christian faith by learning about the Christian Church, how Christ started it, and how it evolved.

How did Christ's teachings, parables, and miracles influence the Church? How did He instruct His disciples and apostles to carry on His work? Was He truly the Son of God, was He man, or was He both?

How did the apostles and early Church Fathers establish means to worship our Lord Jesus Christ so that there could be continuity during the centuries following? Did the apostles follow Jesus's instructions when they established and administered the early Church? And what is the historical connection of the Orthodox Christian Church of today with Christ, the apostles, and the early Church Fathers? These are just a few of the pivotal questions we must ask to gain insight into the origins of our faith.

The Ministry of Jesus

The first and most important foundational truth to faith is believing that Jesus Christ is truly the Son of God. He was man while here on earth so He could set an example for us. He suffered as a human being so our sins could be forgiven and we could embrace salvation, if we so choose. But Jesus Christ as the Son of God is also God. So, we wholeheartedly believe that our Lord Jesus Christ had two natures: divine and human. There is no question, analysis, or rationale here, *only pure faith and belief* in His teachings, instructions, commandments, His many miracles performed, and in His Resurrection. All these events took place over a three-year period and were confined to a small area of this world.

As Jesus ministered, He never traveled more than one hundred miles. His disciples, each ordained to carry on His work, consisted of men like simple fishermen and unpopular tax collectors. Yet, Jesus's teachings, His philosophy, and His example are unprecedented in the history of the human race. Only one who is truly greater than man could have made such an impact on mankind. Scriptures tell us Christ's teachings through the Ten Commandants, the Beatitudes, and His parables. He encourages us to have faith and that we should love our neighbors; He shows us how to ask for forgiveness and how to be forgiving. He also preaches that humility is the forebear of love. Most importantly, he tells us the words that give us salvation: *if we truly, truly believe, we will be saved!*

Jesus began His earthly ministry by fasting for forty days in the wilderness following His baptism. Through this, He taught us that the first step in overcoming the original sin of disobedience to God is by realizing obedience through fasting. Fasting is a way to render one's soul free from the body's constant yearning for satisfaction and gratification.

Almost every great earthly event in the life of Jesus was preceded and followed by prayer. He would withdraw into His Father's presence for prayer and then return into the world strengthened to do His Father's will. Jesus taught us that the fruit of prayer is inner peace, healing power, unlocking the door to the Holy Spirit, union with God, and love. Through Christ, we have access to all such blessings.

Jesus Proclaims the Holy Sacraments

In the Gospels, Jesus gave instructions to His disciples on how to build His Church here on earth. He illustrated to all when He was baptized and told His followers that those entering the Church should be baptized by water in the presence of the Holy Spirit. Later, He gave His disciples bread and wine at the Last Supper, telling them that these were His body and His blood. "Do this in remembrance of me." His first miracle took place at a wedding in Cana, where He taught that the union of man and woman through marriage is sacred in the eyes of God.

Jesus's entire life revolved around ministry. When He returned to earth after the Resurrection, He gave His disciples and apostles instructions on how to continue His work through His Church. Right before His ascension into His Father's Kingdom (forty days after His Resurrection), He told His followers that soon after He went to His Father, the Holy Spirit would come to them and give them the power to go out and teach the Word of God. All this, is of course described in the Acts of the Apostles, which recounts the day of Pentecost (fifty days after the Resurrection), when in an upper room, the Holy Spirit came down to the disciples, administered knowledge and power, and ordained them to go out and teach the Word of God in all languages. There were over three thousand people baptized by Peter that day in Jerusalem. This was the first day of the organized Christian Church. This was the day that would set the pace for generations to come.

It was through this history-changing event that Jesus set forth for His Church the holy sacraments of baptism, communion, marriage, and ordination.

Establishing the Church

If we continue reading in the Acts of the Apostles, we can learn how the apostles of Jesus Christ spread the Word of God throughout the known world and expanded His earthly Church. We learn about the conversion of Paul and how the Lord gave him instructions to spread the gospel to the Gentiles. At this point in history, teaching the Word to the Gentiles was controversial among some apostles, so an Apostolic Synod, the first organized council of the Church, was held in about 50 AD to discuss this issue: Were Gentiles eligible to become followers of Christ?

At that meeting, Paul and Barnabas were successful in convincing the other leaders—including among them James, Peter, and Andrew—how well the Lord was received by the Gentile populous. As a result, all came to a consensus that Gentile believers, even though not of Jewish background, would be included as part of the Body of Christ and not be required to be circumcised. On this day, the Christian Church became a universal Church.

According to documented records, a form of church organization was also discussed at this meeting. This first Apostolic Synod set the precedent for Church leaders to come together to discuss future Church conflicts by *coming to a consensus.*

Establishing the Holy Eucharist Service

As commanded by Christ, the apostles from the beginning carried over from the Last Supper a form of worship service called *Love Feasts,* or *Holy Eucharist,* from the Greek word *efcharistos,* meaning "profound thanks." It began with psalms, hymns, and readings from the Old Testament. The Church leaders would pass on the stories of miracles and teachings of Christ to the worshipers. Jesus's words were then recited: *"Take, eat, this is my body. Drink of it all of you; for this is my blood of the New Testament, which is poured out for the forgiveness of sins"* (Matthew 26:26-28). A prayer was then invoked to change the bread and wine into the body and blood of Christ, as was done by our Lord at the Last Supper. All baptized Christians would then receive the bread and wine as a form of communion with Christ.

Following the writings of the New Testament (between 50 AD and 100 AD), readings from these Holy Scriptures were eventually incorporated into the service. The form of the church service, or Liturgy—from the Greek word *Litourgia,* a common service of a mass of people—was virtually completed by the fourth century. The Liturgy of the Orthodox Church has been essentially unchanged since then.

Development of the Church Doctrines

During the period of Christian persecutions by the Roman Empire (100 AD to 300 AD), the traditions set forth by the apostles and early Church Fathers remained stagnant. Following the legalization of Christianity in 313 AD by the first emperor of New Rome, Constantine the Great, the Church Fathers of that time reconvened and held a series of Church councils for the purpose of continuing to define the dogmas and doctrines on the basis of the Holy Scriptures and the holy traditions established by the original apostles. Between 325 AD and 787 AD, seven ecumenical councils were held.

Due to the transfer of the seat of the Roman Empire from Rome in the west to Byzantium (Constantinople) in the east by Constantine in 321 AD, all ecumenical councils took place in the east. Council interpretations and decisions addressed such important matters as the two natures of Christ, the position of the Theotokos (Virgin Mary), and the role of icons in the Church. The faith and beliefs of the Church were established at the first two councils through the formulation of the Nicene Creed. Christian worship, as well, was defined and established. The twenty-seven books of the New Testament were canonized. The positions of the ranking Church bishops were also established, along with the top five, or *Pentarchy*. These included the bishops of Rome, Constantinople, Antioch, Alexandria, and Jerusalem.

As done in the first Apostolic Synod in 50 AD, all council decisions were by consensus and not by any single leader or bishop. More details related to the Christian Church doctrines are included in Chapter 2.

Divisions in the One, Holy, Apostolic Church

By reading further in history, we find that differences in beliefs and attitudes would soon shape the outcome of the Church. What had once been considered a unified body was quickly dividing because the cultural differences in the Eastern and Western churches—along with the claim of the Bishop of Rome, the Pope, that he was the singular leader of the Church and that he had complete authority and infallibility on all matters of the Church—escalated into major disagreements between the eastern and western geographic areas. The total authority of the popes resulted in a number of implications: their becoming involved in commercial buying and selling; raising large armies to protect their interests; gaining ownership of large territories; and establishing political leadership roles and authority over the western tribal nations. The Eastern Church leaders, on the other hand, concentrated their efforts mainly on ecclesiastical matters and governed the Church by way of a Council of Bishops. These and some major doctrinal differences finally culminated in mutual excommunication, and the *Great Schism of 1054.*

The divergence of the western Church from the dogmas, doctrines, and traditions of the early Church continued on, at last resulting in another split in the form of the Protestant Reformation in the seventeenth century. Soon after, the Roman Catholic Church had a reformation of its own through a series of Vatican councils, initiating a return to the traditions and beliefs of the early Church, which is still continuing today.

In contrast to this return to the early Church, the initial Vatican Council after the Protestant Reformation still confirmed the infallibility of the Pope and strengthened the power, control, and domination of the Pope in all Church matters. The Protestants, on the other hand, discontinued many traditions and sacraments that were previously instituted and commanded by Christ. It's unfortunate that the western Church took the direction it did in the early centuries, because, as we see today, we have three major Christian denominations: the Orthodox, the Catholic, and the Protestant (which has many thousands of denominations of its own). Is such division God's desire?

Less than 30 percent of the world population today is Christian. Is this the way our Lord intended it to be? Chapter 2 further elaborates on the divisions that occurred in the original undivided Christian Church.

Historic Continuity and Sacred Traditions of the Orthodox Christian Church

Many recent theologians, clergymen, and laymen from various faiths have reviewed the history of the Christian Church and come to the conclusion that the Orthodox Christian Church today is the one Christian Church with a true historical connection to the early Church. Over the years, the Orthodox Church has pursued sacramental, doctrinal, and canonical continuity with the ancient undivided Church as it was started by Christ, continued by the apostles, and authoritatively expressed through the original ecumenical councils.

There are numerous important clergymen and theologians who have studied and explored the history of the Christian Church, and as a result they have converted to Orthodoxy. One of the most prominent of these is Dr. Timothy Ware, a highly reputable and former Anglican theologian and clergyman who converted to Orthodoxy in 1959. He subsequently was elevated to bishop (Bishop Kallistos). Those who have heard Bishop Kallistos's stirring lectures, or read his inspiring and instructional articles and books, surely would be impressed with his outstanding intellectual abilities and his strong faith in our Lord Jesus Christ. Yet he is only one of many tools God has used to further His kingdom.

In the early 1950s, a prominent Roman Catholic priest, Father DeBallister, was assigned by the Vatican to research and prepare a history of the Christian Church. During this project, Father DeBallister discovered the significant role of the Orthodox Christian Church in the early Church and its importance in maintaining and carrying on the instructions, teachings, and sacred traditions of Christ and the apostles. Father DeBallister was so impressed and influenced by his research that he converted to Orthodoxy and became an Orthodox priest. My first exposure to Father DeBallister was at a National Conference of the Greek Orthodox Young Adults (GOYA) at Grand Rapids, Michigan in 1959. Father DeBallister described to us his conversion story. While listening to his impassioned speech, for the first time I learned about the historical connection of the Orthodox Church with the original

Church. It was a very exhilarating and enlightening experience for me.

So moved by his rekindled faith, Father DeBallister eventually became a bishop of the Orthodox Church in Mexico. Bishop DeBallister made great strides in his ministry, until a sad turn of events found him shot and killed by an assassin's bullet in the late 1970s.

Many other leaders among men have found the Orthodox traditions fulfilling. Peter Gilchrist and a group of his Protestant-based Campus Crusaders for Christ converted to Orthodoxy in the '80s after writing The History of the Christian Church. This group has been given official status by the Orthodox Church and is known as the Evangelical Orthodox Church of America.

One would be astounded in examining all the priests, ministers, and church groups that have converted to the Orthodox faith in the last few decades. More than fifty-five Episcopalian groups have converted to Orthodoxy. Certainly God has used the faithful pilgrimage of Orthodox believers to advance the work of Christ.

The Spiritual Character and Makeup of the Orthodox Church

The Orthodox Church is autonomous in nature, as opposed to the monolithic authority of the Roman Catholic Church. It is composed of various national churches and holds the original seven ecumenical councils as an important part of the sacred tradition. The Orthodox tradition has permitted certain divergences among the national churches although the doctrines, dogmas, worship, and theology are one. The Church itself is infallible; there is not any one particular leader. A Holy Synod headed by the Patriarch of Constantinople governs it. Decisions at the synod councils are made by consensus.

The foundation of the Church organization is the local church community. The Orthodox Church greatly emphasizes a direct personal relationship with God but does not coerce or force any to do so. The Church believes that God gave each of us a free will and it is up to the individual to decide how to use this gift from God. Orthodoxy strives to help us all find Jesus using our spiritual being and soul through our heart's inner self and not totally through the rational thought process as done in other Christian denominations.

There is little doubt that the Divine Liturgy is the centerpiece of the Orthodox Church. Doctrines, dogmas, and worship have not changed since the beginning. Regarding secular matters, the Orthodox Church has done an excellent job in keeping up with current moral and social issues. It has well-defined stands on abortion, capital punishment, homosexuality, primary sexual relationship between husband and wife to have children, proper sexual relationship between husband and wife to enhance and strengthen the love between them, drugs, violence, today's sexual promiscuity, suicide, euthanasia, and many other significant issues. The Church's strong stand that the unity of the family is the mainstay of a society is applicable to the root of the many ills plaguing our great society today.

In Quest of Jesus by Way of the Divine Liturgy the Holy Eucharist Service

In the ninth century, Prince Vladimir of Russia, still a pagan at that time, set out to establish a national religion for his people. He sent a group of counselors to investigate Judaism, Islam, Rome, and Constantinople to see how each worshiped. When the counselors returned and reported on Constantinople, their comments about the Divine Liturgy at Agia Sophia were: "We did not know whether we were on earth or in heaven." As a result, Vladimir himself visited Constantinople and was baptized. Upon his return to Russia, he started the Russian Orthodox Church, which quickly expanded and grew in popularity throughout Russia. Within a century, Vladimir was proclaimed a saint for his contributions to the Church's movement.

How does one become a part of this sacred celebration and participate in the Holy Eucharist service? How does one achieve that feeling of being on earth yet in heaven, as those counselors felt? An Orthodox Christian must first come to the belief that he is a part of the Church that has maintained the identity of the original Church started by Christ. The Divine Liturgy celebrated in the Orthodox

Church of today has been essentially unchanged since the fourth century, in order to truly express what the apostles and early Church Fathers had originally established. Knowing this, regular attendance to the Liturgy simply isn't enough. It is essential to understand the meanings set forth by all the prayers and hymns and also to truly recognize and comprehend the story that the Liturgy teaches us. The results will be amazing! You will find yourself totally immersed in a faith beyond comprehension.

Liturgy is a remembrance of the life of Christ. Experiencing it takes us back in time to a place where Jesus once treaded. What Jesus said and did two thousand years ago unfolds before your very eyes. You are there when these great events actually happened! You get the feeling of moving toward God and God moving toward you. In the Liturgy, each Epistle reading has a purpose and lesson to it. Each gospel lesson describes an episode in the life of Christ, divine instructions by Christ, or one of Christ's parables.

With understanding the various prayers comes renewed fervor, for the prayers have been written over 1,500 years ago, and yet they are so applicable to today. In reciting the ancient Nicene Creed, you listen in awe at how the total beliefs of the Church could be compressed in such a short statement of faith and possess so much truth.

Then we proceed through the Liturgy and venture through the various events of Christ's life: His ministry, Jesus on the way to Calvary, His death, burial, Resurrection, ascension, and finally His reminder to us of His second coming. Each moment moves us up toward Christ in heaven. All this time, you are personally partaking in these great events. Finally, we end up at the Last Supper! The priest says what Christ Himself said: "*Take, eat; this is my body, which is broken for you for the forgiveness of sins.* … Likewise, *Drink of it all of you; this is my blood of the New Testament, which is shed for you and for many, for the forgiveness of sins.*" At this point, the Holy Spirit descends as it did almost two thousand years ago and changes the bread and wine into the body and blood of Christ.

Throughout the Liturgy, you are constantly learning as the priest recounts the Beatitudes, the Psalms, and other statements of faith. As you meditate the centuries-old hymns of the Church, you increase your knowledge of the Bible, the teachings and traditions of the Church, Christ as humanity's divine friend, how to become more Christ-like, and the Theotokos (the human mother of Christ).

Six times during the Liturgy one has the opportunity to completely and willingly commit oneself to Christ: "*Let us commit ourselves and one another and our whole life to Christ our God.*"

When you leave the church each Sunday after participating in the Liturgy and taking Holy Communion, the worshipers depart feeling one with Christ. On many occasions, I sensed the suffering with Christ followed by a resurrected and renewed spirit. After experiencing this, how can one deny the impact of the Orthodox Divine Liturgy and Holy Eucharistic service? It is truly the centerpiece of the Orthodox Church and places the worshiper on *the path to Jesus*—a path of hope, faith, and love.

There is no doubt that the Holy Spirit empowered the apostles and early Church Fathers in formulating and establishing the Divine Liturgy. The good news is that each of us can freely experience *communion with Christ through the Holy Eucharist.*

For those who take part in the Orthodox Church's beliefs and traditions as they are historically connected to Christ and the apostles, the door to enlightenment opens wide. If you are *truly participating* in the sacraments and in the Divine Liturgy every Sunday and every Feast Day, *reading* the Holy Bible daily, *praying* daily, and maintaining a meaningful *fast*, then you can be certain that you have a *direct path to Jesus.* You will be able to discover the *Logos*—the Word of God and Jesus—by being an active part of a church that has the knowledge, experience, and traditions that can be utilized to help you *live a life in Christ.*

Chapter 2

THE ROLE OF THE ORTHODOX CHURCH IN THE HISTORY OF CHRISTIANITY

INTRODUCTION

What Is a True Church of Christ?

To better grasp the significance of faith, it's important to understand the root (core) words that define it. The word orthodox combines the Greek adjective "*orthos*", which means "right, correct truth," and the noun "*doxa*", which comes from the Greek *doxaso*, "I believe." Hence, orthodox means "right belief" or "true doctrine." In a deeper sense, it denotes "right worship," as doxaso also means "I glorify." Orthodoxy signifies the right belief in the eternal truths as taught by Jesus and the apostles.

The word Greek in Greek Orthodox signifies the contributions of Hellenism to Christianity during the early period of the Church. Hellenism, a cultural movement that followed the conquests of Alexander the Great in the fourth century BC, influenced much of the world's customs and ideals.

How do we know if a church is the true Church of Christ? The history must show that it was founded by Christ and has maintained a living connection over the centuries with the original early Church as established by the apostles according to the instructions of our Lord and Savior Jesus Christ. The Orthodox Church's claim to orthodoxy is founded on apostolic faith based in both the Holy Scriptures and the sacred traditions as interpreted by the Fathers of the Church and as lived out by the whole Church throughout the centuries. The Greek Orthodox Church, also known as the Eastern Orthodox Church, has uninterrupted continuity with the early Church of the apostles. Confident in the truth of our doctrine, we do not deny truth exists in other denominations. However, we claim membership in the Orthodox Christian Church—the One, Holy, Catholic (universal), and Apostolic Church. It is this unified Church that God established almost two thousand years ago and continues even to today.

As we venture on this journey through the history of Christianity, starting from the early Church, we will see that the Orthodox Christian Church is the one Apostolic Church and that our bishops and clergy have uninterrupted succession from the apostles. This is called Apostolic Succession.

The Orthodox Christian Church—A Well-Kept Secret

Many American Christians do not realize the strong sense of history when making first contact with the Eastern Orthodox Church. A contributing factor to misconceptions is the fact that the schools in America concentrate on Western history over international history. For example, school curriculum says very little, if anything at all, about the New Roman Empire or, as it is known more recently, the Byzantine Empire. This vast empire made a significant impact on the future of the entire world. Lasting more than 1,100 years (from 325 to 1453 AD), the Byzantine Empire held the longest form of government in history. It had a form of a congressional government that exists in many countries today. The Byzantine civilization continued the science, math, philosophy, and other important aspects that were initiated by Ancient Greece.

The Byzantine Empire was responsible not only for the establishment of organized Christianity but also for defining the doctrinal, worship, and sacramental aspects of Christianity as we know them today. Most of the art and literature that existed during the Western Renaissance period was inherited from the Byzantine culture. Just as the Orthodox Church maintains continuity with the apostles, it also preserved the liturgical, doctrinal, and sacramental aspects that were established by the apostles and by the Fathers of the Church.

Examples of historical continuity of the Orthodox Church exist throughout the world today. The church at Damascus stands in direct continuity with the Christian congregation that once received Saul of Tarsus and then baptized him as Paul. Similarly, there is historical continuity with the Christians on the island of Cyprus, who were converted by the preaching of Paul and Barnabas. St. Andrew, one of the original twelve apostles, started the church at Antioch, where the followers of our Lord were first called Christians. St. James, the half-brother of Christ, started the church at Byzantium (later called Constantinople). All of these occurrences are described in the Acts of the Apostles and are indisputably a part of the beliefs of all Christian denominations.

Christians who are unfamiliar with the ritual or worship of the Orthodox Church may wonder about the significance of candles and icons, the numerous vestments of the priest, and the fragrant incense, as if it looks like something from a story out of a book or movie. Yet these symbolic icons testify to biblical history, despite what some critics may say. These same critics have no hesitancy in adamantly accepting some of the unfathomable events described in the Holy Scriptures where sticks turn into snakes and where a sea is rolled back. The miracles of our Lord Jesus Christ are of course the ultimate demonstration of God's power, for His works defied reason and science. His miracles are not part of our understanding as to how life and nature behave, as we understand it through our human thought processes. Modern American Christians feel comfortable with the likes of Jacob, Hosea, Elijah, Isaiah, Ezekiel, Daniel, and the apostle John. These men of God and others from the Bible all are an integral part of the Orthodox Christian worship. One can very easily become accustomed to the cultural and religious aspects when it is realized that the traditions of the Orthodox Church, especially in the area of worship, are *a witness to history*—both the miraculous and the ordinary.

THE EARLY CHURCH

God's Covenants and His Chosen People

Prior to the Coming of Christ, God made three covenants with His chosen people—the Semites, also known as the Hebrews, Israelites, or Jews. The first covenant God made was with Adam, in which Adam and Eve could use their free will to develop godliness and assure eternal fellowship with God (Genesis 2:3-19). Orthodox Christians call this eternal fellowship *theosis*. However, Adam and Eve used their gifts of free will to turn away from God, and the result of this choice led to the first sin of mankind.

Many years later, God issued His second spoken covenant with Abraham as described in Genesis 22:1-18. Here God promised to bless Abraham with descendants more numerous than the stars. As the generations of Hebrew people later turned away from Him, God kept reminding His chosen people of the covenant promise through God-ordained prophets and preachers. This is where many of the prophetic books of the Old Testament Bible come from.

God's third covenant was written out for Moses to share with the Jews in the form of the Ten Commandments (Exodus 20:1-17). The Ten Commandments outlined God's rules for living in order to keep His people pure.

History attests to the truth that God worked through the Jews, His chosen people, and promised them that He would send a Messiah to finally establish eternal fellowship with Him and fulfill once and for all the covenant promises. However, the Jews kept drifting away from God. When they rejected Christ, they were no longer the chosen people. The "New Israel" became the believers of Christ who recognized He was the Lord. This new and final covenant continued the same fellowship with God as the previous covenants, but this would be the last, because *He sent His very Son, Jesus Christ, to once and for all join us with God.*

Introduction of Christianity

The ministry of Jesus taught fellowship with God through love. The Old Testament was different in that it focused on the relationship with God through fear. Jesus taught in a spiritual way, because the Kingdom of God was a spiritual kingdom. Religious leaders among the Jews regarded their religion in a legalistic manner rather than a spiritual way. Jesus taught the Fatherhood of God and the brotherhood of man. He taught God's love for man and God's forgiveness of sins. Jesus was truly divine, and the greatest proof of His divine power was His Resurrection, for death could not contain life *and Christ is life*.

The start of the Christian church—the birthday of the church—was Pentecost. Forty days after His Resurrection, Christ assembled with His disciples at the Mount of Olives prior to His Ascension. He commanded them to remain in Jerusalem until the Holy Spirit would empower them to carry out His great commission: "*Go forth and preach to people of all nations baptizing them in the Name of the Father and the Son and the Holy Spirit*" (Luke 24:36-53). Ten days later, or fifty days after the Resurrection, on Pentecost, the Holy Spirit came down upon the disciples and ordained them in the upper room, and the church was established.

The first Christian community was in Jerusalem when, on that day of Pentecost, Peter gave the first sermon on record and three thousand people were baptized into the faith (Acts 2:14-47). St. Paul, who was converted to Christ while on the way to persecute Christians (Acts 9:3-9), was a key leader and missionary of the early Church. Paul went on four missionary journeys from 45 AD to 64 AD. His life was ended as a martyr's death while in Rome in 67 AD. Peter had also been martyred in Rome three years earlier. All the apostles were martyred or executed except for John, who died around 100 AD, after he wrote the Book of Revelation. John lived with the Virgin Mary on the island of Ephesus until her death.

The Christian Church became the universal Church after the Apostolic Synod of 50 AD. (Acts 15:6-29). This was the first Christian conference in history and took place in Jerusalem. All the leaders were present, including Peter and Paul. James—the first bishop of

Jerusalem and the brother (half-brother) of Jesus—was also there to conduct the meeting. Although several matters, including church organization, were discussed, the main issue of the synod was to discuss whether Gentile believers should be obligated to keep the old Jewish law of circumcision in order to become Christian. The final decision to not make circumcision mandatory was made known to all the Christian communities, at that time through letters followed by visits from Paul and others. The significance of the first synod was that the Christian Church became universal for all people. In addition, the Apostolic Synod set the precedent for Church leaders to come together and make important decisions in council and by consensus, as one voice, in future internal and external conflicts.

Initially, Christians worshiped in the synagogues. After the Jewish leaders prohibited the Christians from entering the temples, the worship services were held in private homes. During the persecution of the Christians by the Roman Emperors between 100 AD and 300 AD, services were held in catacombs, cemeteries, basements, and any other secluded area.

Early Christians based the worship service on the Last Supper. The Love Feast or Holy Eucharist service, as it is called, was a dramatic re-enactment of the Last Supper and the life of Christ, just as it is in the Orthodox Divine Liturgy today. The early services covered Jesus's ministry, the Last Supper, and his Resurrection. The leader or clergyman of highest rank would recite Jesus's words, "Take eat, this is my body … Take drink, this is my blood…" and then ask the Holy Spirit to change the offered bread and wine into the body and very blood of Christ in order that all baptized Christians would receive Holy Communion. The services began with psalms, hymns, and readings from the Old Testament. The twenty-seven books of the New Testament, which were written between 50 AD and 100 AD, were officially compiled into one book, or canon, in the fourth century, after which the reading of the Epistles and the Gospel were incorporated into the service.

THE START OF THE BYZANTINE PERIOD—
ESTABLISHMENT AND EXPANSION OF CHRISTIANITY

St. Constantine the Great

At the time of Christ, the Roman Empire was at its zenith. However, the empire began steady decline at the turn of the first century. By the beginning of the fourth century, the empire had been divided into three parts—western, central, and eastern—each with its own ruler. The persecution of the Christians took place before this period (100 AD to 300 AD), when Christianity became illegal. In spite of heavy oppressions, Christian leaders continued the missionary work of Paul and the other apostles as the message of the gospel thrived in Christian centers throughout prominent cities in the empire, including Rome, Jerusalem, Alexandria, and Antioch.

Constantine was the chosen successor to the throne in the western part of the Roman Empire when his father, Philip, was killed in battle in 306 AD. Constantine set out to recapture the middle part of the empire and avenge his father's death. On his way to battle, he saw a cross of light in the sky with the inscription: "In this sign we conquer." Greatly inspired by this, he not only was victorious over the central part of the empire but also conquered the eastern part. Thus, the Roman Empire was once again consolidated and became "The New Roman Empire."

In 313 AD, Constantine issued the Edict of Milan, which ceased the persecution of and tolerated the existence of the Christian Church. Although he was not officially baptized Christian until the day he died, he was considered the first Christian emperor because of his edict and the work he did afterward for the Church. This eventually led to Christianity becoming the official religion of the new Roman Empire and the outlawing of paganism under Emperor Theodosius the Great in 380 AD. Constantine's mother, Helen (St. Helen), was baptized as a Christian early on and was a great influence on St. Constantine.

In 321 AD, Constantine moved the seat of the Roman Empire from Rome to Byzantium in the eastern portion of the empire. Byzantium was later renamed Constantinople after Constantine.

This move led to Byzantium becoming "New Rome" and, thus, the start of the Byzantine period. The term "Byzantine Empire" came into use in more recent times.

Constantinople was strategically located where the east meets the west. It became not only the center of commerce for the New Roman Empire but also the center of the Christian Church. Byzantine history and Church history during this period are so intertwined that they are practically inseparable. The Byzantine period was also marked with outstanding achievements in the areas of philosophy, music, art, architecture, literature, medicine, science, and law. The integration of Christianity and Hellenism also took place. As Christianity felt cultural influence over the years, Hellenistic traditions left an imprint on the faith.

Christianity and Hellenism

The roots of Western civilization are Judeo-Christian and Greco-Roman, which is to say there would be no west if the Jews and Greeks had not existed. Athens was the first civilization to establish a full democracy and ushered in the Golden Age of Greece.

When Alexander conquered the known world, he spread the spirit of Hellenism throughout his realm. During the period of Alexander the Great, the Greek language, or Hellenism, became the common, international language reaching from Sicily to the Persian Gulf. Under Roman domination, Greek culture became the backbone of the Roman Empire and Greek remained the common language of the three continents that formed the Mediterranean basin. Even the New Testament and St. Paul's Epistle to the Romans were written in Greek.

Greek philosophy established through the great philosophers like Socrates, Plato, and Aristotle became a key part of Christian preaching. Socrates had gone to his death proclaiming the existence and immortality of the soul. Plato, a disciple of Socrates, elaborated on a theory of objectivity and universality of truth. Then, his disciple, Aristotle, developed rules for the proper use of reason. Most Greek philosophers agreed that, at the heart of all things, there is a logos ("word") that gives intelligibility and being to everything.

Embracing these tenants, Christian preachers gave these classical Greek concepts new content and meaning in Christ.

THE DEVELOPMENT OF CHRISTIAN CHURCH DOCTRINES AND WORSHIP

This next section discusses the doctrines and beliefs of the Christian Church that were established during the Byzantine period, especially as a result of the seven ecumenical councils. Included in the discussion is Church worship, commonly known as the Divine Liturgy.

The Seven Ecumenical Councils

The pattern of the Church councils to determine accepted traditions and beliefs was already established by the turn of the fourth century AD, starting with the Apostolic Synod in 50 AD. In 325 AD, Constantine the Great summoned a Church council at the city of Nicea to deal with the erroneous teaching of Arius and to set the date to celebrate Easter. Arius taught that if Jesus was born, there must have been a time when He did not exist. Therefore, there must have been a time when Jesus was not God. Because the council was judged to speak for the whole Church and not just for one region, it received the name "ecumenical," meaning "worldwide." The Council of Nicea was the first of a total of seven ecumenical councils held during the Byzantine period. These councils, along with the major Church issues that were resolved in each, are summarized below:

I. Council of Nicea, 325 AD – Condemnation of Arianism; affirmed the full divinity of Christ. Established the date of Easter. Prepared the composition of the first part of the Nicene Creed. Accepted the instructions and procedures set forth by the original apostles. Started the discussion of the organizational structure of the Christian Church.

II. Council of Constantinople, 381 AD – Confirmed the Holy Trinity; that Father, Son, and Holy Spirit are equal and one. Completed the remaining five articles of the Nicene Creed. Established the rank of the Patriarch of Constantinople; "The Bishop of Constantinople shall rank next to the Bishop of Rome, because Constantinople is the new Rome."

III. Council of Ephesus, 431 AD – Affirmed the personality of Jesus Christ as divine. Even though Jesus Christ was complete God and complete man, the union between His divine nature and human nature were such that one did not disturb the other. Established that the Virgin Mary was truly *Theotokos*, because she received and gave birth to Jesus, the Son of God.

IV. Council of Chalcedon, 451 AD – Clarified the two equal natures of Christ. Affirmed He became incarnate (was embodied in flesh; assumed a living form) through the Virgin Mary, who is truly *Theotokos* and Mother of God. Established the Pentarchy Rank for the organization of the Church. The Pentarchy included the rank of the bishops for the five major Christian centers at that time. The Bishop of Rome was first among equals, with the Bishop of Constantinople ranking next. These were followed by Alexandria, Antioch, and Jerusalem. The council established that all five were equal with regard to apostolic succession.

V. Constantinople, 553 AD – Declared once and for all the teachings of the Church regarding the two natures of Jesus Christ.

VI. Constantinople, 680 AD – Affirmed that possessing two natures, Jesus Christ necessarily possesses two integral wills. Each nature exercises its own free will.

VII. Nicea, 787 AD – Affirmed the value of *venerating* the holy images (icons) of Christ and the saints. The seventh ecumenical council was the last true ecumenical council convened, due to the eventual separation of the Eastern and Western churches in 1054 AD. The Eastern Orthodox Church, as of today, closely follows the decisions and traditions of the first seven ecumenical councils.

The Divine Liturgy

The greatest and most classic example of Christian literature during the Golden Age of Byzantium was the formation and final development of the Divine Liturgy. The early Eucharistic service (Divine Liturgy) were held by the early Christians, first in synagogues, then in homes, and later in catacombs during times of the persecution. The formation and structure of the Eucharist continued to develop so that by the Peace of the Church (313 AD) the Divine Liturgy had been fairly well established. Various documents from that early Church period describe in detail the Liturgies of those times, which are discussed in Chapter 5. There were, however, different styles or rites that developed in the east versus the west.

The Byzantine Liturgy was a Eucharistic service that combined the teachings and practices and rites of Jerusalem, Antioch, and Constantinople. By the beginning of the sixth century, the Byzantine Liturgy embraced four styles: Liturgy of St. John Chrysostom (the Liturgy normally used today); Liturgy of St. Basil (Liturgy used on Sundays during Lent); Liturgy of St. James (used twice a year); and the Liturgy of the Pre-sanctified Gifts (today celebrated every Wednesday during Lent). The Pre-sanctified Liturgy combines the first half of a vesper, or evening service, and the second half of the Eucharist without the consecration of the holy gifts. The consecration takes place at the Liturgy of the previous Sunday. The Orthodox Church has consistently maintained the integrity of the Byzantine Liturgy throughout the centuries.

In the west, there was no authoritatively fixed Liturgy until after the sixteenth century Protestant Reformation. Unlike in the east, there was a lack of unity in the west due to the early century invasions and conquering of territories by tribes such as the Goths (Spain), Gauls (France), and Anglo-Saxons (Britain). As a result of fluctuating political domination, various types of liturgies evolved in different territories. When the western Church finally established a Roman rite, it was altered many times between the sixth to the sixteenth centuries.

Since Vatican II Council (1965), the Roman Catholic Church has embarked on a liturgical renewal to restore the ancient Roman rite, which is in many ways similar to the Orthodox Liturgy of today. Protestant scholars join in this liturgical renewal as liturgical scholars in both the Roman Catholic Church and Protestant churches have begun to look to the ancient Church for insight in making the Liturgy relevant. Their discoveries show that the Orthodox Church has maintained the corporate worship in the Divine Liturgy. The significance of this is Orthodox Divine Liturgy is today relevant and celebrated the same at all times by all Eastern Orthodox churches throughout the world.

Even though the Roman Catholic and Protestant liturgical scholars are beginning to realize the relevancy of the Orthodox Liturgy, many Orthodox Christians at times do not. It is important for Orthodox followers to recognize the value of the Liturgy, then attend and *participate* regularly in the Divine Liturgy. We must recognize that the Divine Liturgy is a remembrance of our Lord and Savior Jesus Christ. What Jesus said and did almost two thousand years ago happens again before our eyes, and it is our joy to partake in this. We are actually there when these great events happened! Through the Eucharist, the Lord is born in us. By attending and participating in the Divine Liturgy every Sunday and on Feast Days, we are in turn resurrected through Jesus Christ; we are born again.

Other Differences between East and West

When Constantine moved the capital from Rome to Byzantium, this began a period of estrangement between the east and west. Differences arose because of geographical, political, cultural, and religious reasons. In 527 AD, Justinian, emperor in the east, sent armies to Western Europe and North Africa to once again solidify the empire. This led to the period of the Dark Ages in the west. Justinian reigned victorious, but before he could solidify the empire, the bubonic plague spread throughout Constantinople into Western Europe, wiping out half of the population. This not only diminished the population but also the economy. After Justinian's death, it was decided by the new emperor that the armies in Western Europe could not be sustained, so they were withdrawn and returned to Constantinople. Due to this retreat, the east was considerably weakened and Western Europe furthered the Dark Ages to a greater extent.

The monolithic authority of the Pope in the west was also a factor in dividing the east and the west. Differences became evident starting in the sixth century and continued to the point that there was a permanent split, or schism, between the Eastern and Western churches in 1054 AD. The Great Schism, as it was known, is discussed in detail in the subsequent chapter.

ANCIENT PATRIARCHATES AND NATIONAL ORTHODOX CHURCHES

Christianity Spreads to the Slavic Nations

The Slavs were tribes of Eastern Europe with origins dating as far back as a few centuries BC. The conversion of the Slavs, who were north of Byzantium, to Christianity began in the ninth century and continued to spread geographically. In 863, Patriarch Photius decided to send priests and missionaries to teach Christianity to the Slavs in their own language. Photius sent two brothers, Cyril and Methodius, who were natives of Thessalonica. During their childhood, they had learned the dialect of the Slavs and could speak it fluently. The accomplishments of Saints Cyril and Methodius were outstanding as they took the theology, philosophy, and traditions of Byzantium and Christianized the unknown northern Slavic states. They created a Slavonic alphabet and translated the liturgical books and the Bible into a language that was intelligible to the Slavs. That language has remained the liturgical language for all the Slavic churches to this day.

The eastern Slavic nations that converted to Christianity remained part of the Eastern Orthodox Church, including Serbia, Rumania, Bulgaria, and Russia. These churches, along with Greece, formed the nucleus of the group of national churches that comprise the Eastern Orthodox Church today. These churches eventually became autocephalous, or independent administratively, from the Patriarch of Constantinople.

The Growth of National Orthodox Churches

The following list composes the national Orthodox churches and their origins:

1. Bulgarian Orthodox Church – Conversion to Orthodox Christianity started in 863. Bulgaria became the first independent national church of the Slavs around 1250 AD. Patriarchal rank was granted to the Bishop of Sophia and all Bulgaria (who later became a Patriarchate and autocephalous). The Turks successfully invaded Bulgaria in the fifteenth century, and they remained under the Turkish rule until the nineteenth century.

2. Serbian Orthodox Church – Christianity was introduced to the Serbs late in the ninth century by Saints Cyril and Methodius. In spite of attempts by the Pope to convert the Serbs to Rome, the Serbs remained loyal to Constantinople. However, the Croatian territory became Roman Catholic when the Pope declared one of the Croatian chieftans to be the Bishop of Croatia. In 1221, the Ecumenical Patriarch of Constantinople recognized the Serbian church as an independent church, a new National Serbian Orthodox Church or patriarchate. Serbia was also under the rule of the Ottoman Turks from the fifteenth to the nineteenth century.

3. Rumanian Orthodox Church – The conversion of the Rumanians to Orthodoxy took place in the twelfth century. They remained under the Ecumenical Patriarch of Constantinople until 1925, when the patriarch elevated Rumania to a patriarchate with its seat in Bucharest. They were also under the rule of the Turks from the fifteenth to the nineteenth century.

4. Ukrainian Orthodox Church – The churches of Western Poland, Lithuania, and the Ukraine were originally under the Patriarch of Constantinople. However, local political rulers, because of proximity to the west, pressured the bishops in those areas to sign an act of union with Rome in 1596. These became known as the *Uniate* Churches, Latin for "union." They were later known as the Greek

Catholic or Byzantine Rite Church, as they were allowed to maintain the Byzantine Liturgy and traditions. This is a major conflict and controversy between the Orthodox and Catholic churches even today.

A significant group of Ukrainian bishops, priests, and layman remained Orthodox. In 1686, Ukraine was annexed by Russia and the Ukraine church was put under the jurisdiction of the Church of Russia.

5. **Russian Orthodox Church** – Russia obtained the Slavonic language as a result of Saints Cyril and Methodius. The prime mover of Russia's conversion to Orthodoxy, however, was Saint Vladimir when Prince Vladimir sent a group of counselors to each of the major religious bodies (Judaism, Islam, Rome, and Constantinople) to see how they actually worshiped. When the counselors returned from Constantinople remarking about the Divine Liturgy at St. Sophia, they said, *"We did not know whether we were on earth or in Heaven. For on earth there is no such splendor or such beauty, and we are at a loss how to describe it. We know only that God dwells there among men, and their service is more virtual and fairer than the ceremonies of other nations. For we cannot forget that beauty."* As a result, Vladimir visited Constantinople himself and was baptized in 987 AD. Russia was formally converted to Orthodoxy.

The greatest strides of Orthodoxy were made in Russia, particularly during the Ottoman conquest of Greece and the Balkan countries. They achieved a remarkable spiritual unity among the different national and ethnic groups in Russia. Russia became a patriarchate in 1589.

6. **The Church of Greece** – For over 400 years, Greece under Turkish rule offered a buffer between the Turks and the Italians, French, Spanish, and other western nations. Greece was heroic in their determination in sustaining Orthodoxy and Greek traditions against insurmountable odds under Turkish domination. This heroism is what unified them and finally inspired them under the leadership of the Church to revolt against the Turks, which led to

the downfall of the Ottoman Empire and eventual independence of the remaining Orthodox nations.

The Greek Orthodox Church was under the jurisdiction of the Ecumenical Patriarch in Constantinople until 1850, when it was made autocephalous (self-governing). Greece is not at this time a patriarchate and is ruled by an archbishop.

7. **Other Orthodox Churches** – Other Orthodox churches, which are autocephalous and ruled by a metropolitan or an archbishop, are the churches of Cyprus and Czechoslovakia. The Church of Finland is autonomous, self-governing in most respects, but has not reached full independence to be named autocephalous. The Orthodox Church in America is in a unique situation, which has never before existed in the history of the Orthodox Church. It has expanded to the point of becoming autocephalous, but it has been named as a synodal church and is under the jurisdiction of the Patriarch of Constantinople.

8. **The Ancient Patriarchates** – Along with Constantinople, the remaining ancient patriarchates, which occupy a special position in the Orthodox Church, are the churches of Alexandria, Antioch, and Jerusalem. These ancient churches rank first in honor. This position is still maintained in spite of their small size.

ORTHODOX CHRISTIANITY COMES TO AMERICA

The foundation for the Eastern Orthodox Church in America was laid when a Russian Orthodox mission from Valasin Monastery was sent to Alaska in 1794. During the first two years after arriving, the missionaries baptized twelve thousand natives and built several chapels. The Russian missionaries then continued southward to the California territory, where the first Orthodox chapel was built at Fort Ross in 1812, just north of San Francisco. A Russian, Bishop Innocent, was most instrumental in the spread of Orthodoxy on the northwestern tip of North America in the mid 1800s.

The Greek Orthodox Church in America

The first record of Greeks on American soil points back to 1767, when the Colony of Smyrna was founded on the eastern side of the Florida coastline. The workers migrated north to St. Augustine in 1793. Although there were about one hundred Greek residents, there is no record of any organization of a church community. The Greek Orthodox Archdiocese has constructed the St. Photius Shrine Chapel at St. Augustine to commemorate the first known Greek immigrants to the American continent.

The first Greek Orthodox Church in America was Holy Trinity, located in New Orleans, built in 1866. Other parishes were organized and churches constructed in the 1890s with the emergence of the immigration period (such as Holy Trinity, New York, and Holy Trinity, Chicago, in 1892). By the end of the first decade of the twentieth century, there were over fifty Greek Orthodox parishes throughout America. Today there are over 550 parishes in the United States as well as Greek Orthodox communities in Canada, Mexico, and South America.

The Greek Orthodox Archdiocese of North and South America

With the emergence of Greek immigrants and the presence of the Greek Orthodox Church in America, the transition and adjustment ended up a difficult one. At first, the churches fell under the jurisdiction of the Ecumenical Patriarchate of Constantinople. However, in March of 1908, the patriarch transferred the jurisdiction over to the Holy Synod of the Church of Greece. The problems of uniformity and cooperation of the churches became complex and difficult in the next few years due to the lack of a strong religious leader in this country and to the political problems that arose in Greece as a result of the First World War. In 1922. the jurisdiction of the churches was returned to the Ecumenical Patriarchate of Constantinople.

Eight years later, in 1930, the Archdiocese of North and South America was organized by the ecumenical patriarchate and the Holy Synod of Greece, with one archbishop and four assisting bishops for the four Diocesan Districts New York, Chicago, Boston, and

San Francisco. The Metropolitan Bishop of Corfu, Athenagoras, was appointed as the new archbishop of the Greek Archdiocese of North and South America. During his term of office, he brought several dissident churches back to the archdiocese and founded numerous new parishes, the Ladies Philoptochos Societies, Holy Cross Seminary, St. Basil's Academy for children, the monthly publication *The Orthodox Observer,* and mission churches in Latin and South America. On November 1, 1948, Archbishop Athenagoras was elected Ecumenical Patriarch of Constantinople. He died at the ripe age of eighty-six on July 7, 1972 and was succeeded by Demetrios I. Following his untimely death in 1992, Demetrios I was succeeded by Bartholomew, the current Patriarch of Constantinople.

Following his appointment as patriarch, Archbishop Athenagoras was succeeded as leader of the archdiocese in the Americas by Archbishop Michael, who was a brilliant scholar and theologian. He greatly enhanced the prestige of Orthodoxy in America. In addition to his administrative achievements, he founded G.O.Y.A., the Home for the Aged in Yonkers, N.Y., created a public relations department, and promoted national recognition of Eastern Orthodoxy as a major faith in America. Archbishop Michael joined the National Council of Churches of America and became one of the five presidents of the World Council of Churches Presidium. He was the first Orthodox prelate to deliver an invocation at a presidential inauguration in January 1957. Archbishop Michael passed away in 1959 and was laid to rest on the grounds of St. Basil Academy.

Following in Archbishop Michael's footsteps, Archbishop Iakovos was enthroned as Archbishop of the Americas on April 1, 1959. He strengthened and reshaped American Orthodoxy and is considered the most influential Orthodox prelate in America. Archbishop Iakovos gave the inaugural invocation for President John F. Kennedy and was active in the Civil Rights and other human rights movements in this country. Under his administration, a new Constitution for the Archdiocese was written, and at his initiative, the archdiocese was restructured and chartered as a Synodal Church in 1974. Archbishop Iakovos did much to promote cooperation and interaction among the various ethnic Orthodox churches in

America. His Eminence organized SCOBA in 1960, the Council of Orthodox Bishops of America, in an attempt to strengthen the interaction of all the Orthodox churches and work toward unifying the churches to form one Orthodox Church in America. Archbishop Iakovos retired in 1996. Archbishop Spyriodon, who served until 1999, replaced him. His Eminence, Archbishop Demetrios, was appointed in 1999 and is currently serving.

Organization became key to the growth of the Orthodox Church in America. In December of 2002, the Holy Synod of the Patriarchate of Constantinople granted a new charter to the Greek Orthodox Church in America. The dioceses were elevated to metropolises and the hierarchs of the dioceses were all elevated as metropolitans of their respective metropolises. The new Greek Archdiocese of America consists of the Archdiocesan District of New York with eight metropolises—New Jersey, Chicago, Atlanta, Detroit, San Francisco, Pittsburgh, Boston, and Denver. The archbishop and the Synod of Bishops, which is composed of the bishops who oversee the ministry of the metropolises, govern the new archdiocese.

Slavic and Other Orthodox Churches in America

As the gates to America opened, people flooded the thriving country in search of the American dream. Among the masses were those rooted in the Slavic churches, including the Russian Church, and evolution proved inevitable in the 1920s, during the immigration periods for those countries, and after the Russian Revolution. As a result of objections to the co-existence of the Russian Orthodox Church with the Russian Communist Government, three different Russian Orthodox groups evolved. These are:

1. Russian Orthodox Synodal Church outside of Russia – under the Patriarch of Constantinople

2. Russian Orthodox Greek Catholic Church –the largest in membership and under the Patriarchate of Moscow

3. Russian Orthodox Patriarchal Church – under Moscow

The Russian Church in America is in a similar situation that the Greek Orthodox Church was in during the 1920s and early 1930s.

Perhaps these problems can be worked out with the downfall of the Communist government in Russia, similar to what happened to the Greek Orthodox Church in the 1930s and 1940s.

Other Slavic churches in America include the Ukrainian Church, Bulgarian Church, Serbian Church, Rumanian Church, Syrian or Antiochan Church, American Carpatho-Russian Orthodox Greek Catholic Church, and Albanian Church.

The Evangelical Orthodox Church was started in 1986 when a group of staff members of the Campus Crusades for Christ (Protestant)—after a historical, doctrinal, and liturgical search and study—organized the church and subsequently became under the jurisdiction of the Antiochian Church. They have taken the challenge to evangelize non-Orthodox Americans to the Orthodox Church.

Should There Be a Pan-Orthodox Church in America?

Orthodox Christians, by and large, who immigrated to America, came from national churches abroad. Thus, the early churches that were formed were in a broad sense immigrant churches. It was only natural they organize under their national churches and/or patriarchates. As time ebbed, for one reason or another, disagreements and divisions emerged among individual jurisdictions. It is interesting to note that this was the first time in the history of the Orthodox Church when churches were started in a new country and the natural language of that country wasn't used for the liturgical language.

In order to cope, and at the same time project some type of unity between the various Orthodox jurisdictions, the Standing Conference of Canonical Orthodox Bishops in America (SCOBA) was organized by His Eminence, Archbishop Iakovos, in 1960. SCOBA consists of the leading bishops of each canonical jurisdiction and acts as a clearinghouse to focus the efforts of the Orthodox Church at large on common concerns and to avoid overlapping and duplication of the services. Special services are devoted to college campus work, Christian education, military, and ecumenical relations.

His Eminence also considered SCOBA as a first step in combining all the ethnic Orthodox churches into one Church with a common language. However, progress over the years in accomplishing this was slow, as the Patriarch of Constantinople rejected the effort toward unity in the '90s. It's not clear as to why this was not acceptable to the Ecumenical Patriarch of Constantinople, because it would have been in conjunction with the joint sanction, blessing, and approval of all the other Orthodox jurisdictional heads from which each of the Orthodox bodies in America stems. Efforts should continue to merge all the Orthodox churches in America into a union of churches by SCOBA, for it's a goal worthy of the investment and should be a major goal for the leadership of the Greek Orthodox Church to accomplish this.

Chapter 3

PATH OF THE ROMAN CATHOLIC CHURCH PURSUANT TO THE DIVISION OF EAST AND WEST AND PROTESTANT REFORMATION

SEPARATION OF EAST AND WEST

Differences Arise

In the eastern part of the Roman Empire, Constantinople, which had been made the "New Rome" in 321 AD, was also the center of commerce for the whole empire. In the east, philosophy, science, literature, and art of Ancient Greece (Hellenism) steadily developed. All seven ecumenical councils, which established Christian doctrines and beliefs, were held in the east. Unity was maintained in the east under one central political authority, the emperor, who was greatly involved in the Church. Under this political and cultural environment, the Church leaders were able to attend mostly to Church matters. The Eastern bishops believed in ecclesiastical rank of bishops, as related to the importance of the city, but equal in rank regarding apostolic succession as bishops traced their history to biblical apostles. Thus, they did not believe in the supremacy of any one bishop, but made Church decisions by consensus through Church councils.

In the west, Rome isolated itself from the eastern part of the New Roman Empire following the transfer of the seat of the empire from Rome to Constantinople. Invasion by the northern tribes eventually resulted in the formation of separate tribal states consisting of England, France, Italy, North Africa, and Spain. As a result of this weakening of central political authority in the west, the Bishop of Rome began to emerge as an important central leader, both politically and religiously. This eventually led to the rise of the Papal State or primacy of the Pope. The Bishop of Rome became the central figure of leadership for the tribal kingdoms This also was the beginning of moral deterioration in the Western Church of Rome.

Political Separation

By the ninth century, the tribal states in the west became known as the Holy Roman Empire. During this period, the New Roman Empire, or Byzantine Empire, in the east flourished economically and culturally. The Eastern Church was expanded into the Slavic States of Eastern Europe, including Bulgaria, Serbia, Ukraine, Russia, and Rumania. At the same time, the Western Church expanded to the non-Slavic states of Europe, including Germany, Czechoslovakia, Hungary, and Croatia. This division is even evident today, and the animosity between some states, as initiated over ten centuries ago, still exists, such as tensions between Serbia and Croatia.

Cultural Differences

There was a fundamental difference in Greek and Latin temperaments. Up to the year 200 AD, Greek was the language of the Church in both east and west. With the turn of the third century, Latin became the spoken language of the west while Greek remained the language in the east.

The east was interested in philosophy, speculative thought, and mysticism inherited from the Hellenistic period. The west was more concerned with concise, legalistic, and institutional practices inherited from the Romans. The differences in philosophies were reflected in the type of church organizations that were structured in the east and west. The east developed into a group of national churches and ancient patriarchates that were autocephalous, each with its own patriarch. The Patriarch of Constantinople is the first among equals and decisions are made by consensus via Church councils. The west differs in that there is a central authority in the form of the Pope, who is the supreme head of the Church, is infallible, and makes decisions on all Church matters.

Papal Supremacy

One of the major differences that caused the eventual separation of the east and west was the claim of the Bishop of Rome: he sought papal supremacy. As the Bishop of Rome emerged as a central figure in the west, both religiously and politically, he became increasingly powerful. This power was partly based on two false documents. The first document was called "The Donation of Constantine," which was later proven to be a forgery, claiming that Constantine donated sizeable strips of land in Italy and Sicily to the Bishop of Rome. The second claim was based on the false claims of the Decretals of Isidore, documents that rejected the documents of the apostles, which were accepted by the first ecumenical council. The documents of the apostles presented a series of instructions pertaining to sacraments, doctrines, and administrative procedures. The Decretals of Isidore claimed that the Bishop of Rome, or Pope, had supreme authority from the beginning and required all bishops to appeal directly to the Pope for approval of all matters. These two false documents allegedly gave the Bishop of Rome the title of "Pontiff" and Father of the Universe. The Bishop of Rome's authority continued to expand and eventually led to the Popes becoming engaged in buying, selling, and shipping commodities as well as going to war with their own armies to protect their lands and businesses. In contrast, the Church leaders in the east, including the Bishop of Constantinople, concentrated solely on Church matters and made Church decisions by consensus through councils, similar to the apostles in their Apostolic Synod of 50 AD.

The Pope's claim of total authority was reinforced in the west on the basis of the Petrine Promise and the Filioque Clause. The Popes considered the passage from Matthew 16:13-19, "Upon this rock I will build my Church" as Jesus's personal call to Peter to succeed Him and be God's representative on earth. The Popes justified this by claiming that Peter was the first Bishop of Rome, and thus they were Jesus's representatives on earth. Ancient Church records show that Peter was the first bishop in several areas such as Antioch and Rome, until he designated his successors in those places as the "first" bishop.

The Orthodox Church believes that when St. Peter declared to Jesus Christ that He is the Son of God, he was declared by Jesus to be the rock (petra) of the Church. When Peter spoke, he represented all the disciples, and when Jesus answered him, He spoke not only to all the disciples but to all the successive bishops of the Church throughout all the centuries.

In the seventh century, the Latin phase *Filioque* ("and the Son") was added in the Latin Creed to the original phrase in the Nicene Creed (issued by the first and second ecumenical councils): "and I believe in the Holy Spirit, the Lord, the Giver of Life, who proceeds from the Father." This addition of "and the Son" to "who proceeds from the Father" implies that Jesus can send the Holy Spirit even though Jesus promised His disciples after the Resurrection that, "He would ask God the Father to send the Holy Spirit at the appointed time" (Acts 1:4). The Filioque Clause with the Petrine Promise implied that if Jesus can send the Holy Spirit, and Jesus asked Peter to be His vicar (His representative on earth) then Peter too can send the Holy Spirit, as can each consecutive Bishop of Rome. If the Bishop of Rome truly has this sole power, then he is beyond reproach and infallible in all matters. This false teaching strengthened the position of authority of the Pope in the west to an unbelievable degree.

The Great Schism

By the early tenth century, the false notion of the papal supremacy became fixed in the west. When an attempt was made by Rome to impose this supremacy on the Patriarch of Constantinople, it resulted in the Great Schism of 1054 AD. The divide came about when Pope Leo IX's representatives presented a bull of excommunication to Patriarch Michael Cerularius of Constantinople while he was celebrating the Divine Liturgy in St. Sophia. Several days later, the patriarch countered with the excommunication of the Pope's representatives following a council of Eastern bishops in Constantinople.

Since that unfortunate and tragic incident there have been numerous attempts to reunite the east and west. Out of all of them, only three led to a form of union, but the people in the east did not accept the terms. A major factor that impacted the failure of union was the consequences from the Crusades. Union presented countless stumbling blocks between Roman Catholics and Orthodox including several doctrinal and organizational aspects. The greatest obstacle, however, remains the primacy of the Pope, which is misconstrued to mean a supremacy and infallibility of the Bishop of Rome. The Orthodox Church recognizes the primacy of *honor* given to the Bishop of Rome by the early Church; however, it rejects the *supremacy* and *infallibility* demanded by the Roman Catholic Church.

The excommunication by the Pope of Rome and counter-excommunication by the Patriarch of Constantinople in 1054 AD were mutually lifted by Patriarch Athenagoras and Pope Paul VI in 1965. Since then, discussions regarding the differences between the two churches have been held. However, at this time there is no apparent indication of progress toward a union of the two Christian churches. No matter what cultural, political, and religious events occurred throughout history, one fact remains: the Orthodox Church has maintained and not distorted the basic doctrines of the One, Holy, Catholic (universal), and Apostolic Church handed down from Jesus Christ and His apostles.

END OF THE BYZANTINE PERIOD

The beginning of the eighth century found the Byzantine Empire in much danger from the Islamic onslaught that had been occurring. The Byzantine political and Church leaders managed to save the empire time and time again, but the weakening of the empire by the Crusades was instrumental in finally allowing the conquest of Constantinople by the Ottoman Turk Moslems in 1453 AD.

The Rise of Islam

The Arabs were people of Semitic origin (same as the Jews) who occupied the Arabian Peninsula long before the coming of Christianity. The early religion of the Arabs was a primitive one that consisted of worshiping idols and other objects, such as trees. The Arab nomadic tribes finally accepted monotheism by the sixth century under the influence of Judaism and Christianity. One man, however, was solely responsible for the unification of the Arabian tribes, when he founded a world religion and became prophet and chief of a political nation called Islam. His name was Muhammad.

Muhammad was born in 570 AD and grew up in Mecca. Surrounded by Christians and Jews, he developed distaste for idol worship and in time he acquired a growing respect for monotheism. Muhammad had numerous visions, the first of which was of the Archangel Gabriel, who told him to "recite.". His sayings grew out of these visions and were eventually written down by his disciples in the Islamic Bible or Koran.

The prophet Muhammad gained a large following by starting a series of holy wars, which led to the national conquest of the Arabian Peninsula. By the seventh and eighth centuries, the Arabs had expanded their territories to include Syria, Palestine (the Holy Land), Egypt, and North Africa. The more they grew, the more they became a direct threat to Constantinople and the Byzantine Empire. The followers of Islam, called Moslems, believe Allah (the same as the Christian and Jewish God) is the one and only God. The differences, however, begin to reveal themselves in the details of theology. They believe that the Christian doctrine of the Holy Trinity is polytheistic. Islam reveres all the prophets from Abraham to Christ, but believes that Muhammad was the last and greatest of all prophets. They implemented no organized priesthood or sacraments. There are a number of ritualistic observances, such as prayers five times a day, fasting, almsgiving, and pilgrimages to the holy city of Mecca and to Jerusalem, second to Mecca. The utterances of Muhammad, as expressed in the Koran, represent the final and absolute expression of the will of God, or Allah. The Koran confirms the truths of the Old (Torah) and New Testaments by stating that the righteous will have rewards in heaven and the wicked will burn in hell on the day of Final Judgment. The Koran mentions the birth, death, and resurrection of Jesus.

Contrary to what occurs in today's political climate, the Koran states to fight only against those who fight against Allah and an individual, but one should not start hostilities. The word *Islam* means "submission to God" and a Moslem is one who submits. Islam is more than a religion; it is a way of life. To the believer, religion and life, faith and politics are all one and the same.

Consequences of the Crusades

In the latter part of the eleventh century, Pope Urban II promoted the first Crusade to free the Holy Lands from the Arabs. In traveling from Western Europe to the Holy Lands, the Crusaders trekked through the east. As they encountered Eastern clergyman enroot, the Crusaders looked upon them as heretics, making every possible attempt to Latinize the people to the point of replacing the Eastern clergy with Latin clergy. The greatest blow struck to the east took place in 1204 AD, when the fourth Crusade turned to Constantinople instead of Jerusalem. The Crusaders broke into the city on Good Friday and for three days savagely attacked and looted Constantinople. Not only were Orthodox clergy killed, but as a result of the ransacking, mankind lost some of its greatest masterpieces of ecclesiastical articles, iconography, and library collections. This attack on Constantinople was one of the major disasters of Christian history.

The Latin conquerors of Constantinople replaced the patriarch with a Latin prelate,
similar to the role of a bishop, then did the same in Antioch and Jerusalem. The Latin Crusaders stayed for about sixty years, when a new Byzantine emperor recaptured Constantinople and restored Eastern Patriarchs to Constantinople, Antioch, and Jerusalem. The Crusades temporary conquest of Constantinople not only made the schism between east and west that had occurred two hundred years before more complete, but it also undermined the resistance of the

Byzantines against the Moslems. This eventually led to the conquest of Constantinople by the Ottoman Turks.

The Fall of Constantinople

Following the trail of conquests by Islam in Egypt, North Africa, and parts of Europe, the Moslems were constantly menacing Constantinople. Time and time again, the Byzantine emperors successfully defended the city and held the Moslems back. However, after the separation of the east and west coupled with the Crusades, Muhammad II, the Turkish emperor, gathered a huge army and planned his strategy the latter part of 1452 to attack Constantinople. Muhammad II laid siege to the city in the spring of 1453. In spite of eight weeks of constant battering of the city's protective walls with cannons, and several attacks by the Turkish troops, the Greek Byzantines fought bravely. The city finally fell in the end of May in 1453. As a result of the fall of Constantinople, all of Eastern Christendom (including Greece, Rumania, Bulgaria, Serbia, and others), with the exception of Russia, subsequently fell under the Turkish yoke. Nevertheless, the Eastern Orthodox Church remained strong during the four hundred years of tyranny and bondage under the Turkish Ottoman Empire. In fact, it was the Church that perpetuated both the faith and the spirit of liberation, which ultimately came about in the nineteenth century.

DECLINE IN THE WESTERN ROMAN CATHOLIC CHURCH AND THE PROTESTANT MOVEMENT

Deterioration in the Western Church

Following the Fourth Crusades in the thirteenth century, the Western Church of Rome continued their moral deterioration. The basis for this decline was laid long before the Crusades when the Pope secured the power and supremacy over the Church during the formation of the tribal states. By the Fourth Crusades, the Church also had gotten involved in feudalism, wars, and commerce, which contributed to the ethical decline. After the Crusades, two schools of thought emerged, further corroding the moral fiber of the Western Church. These were Scholasticism and Humanism.

Scholasticism attempted to rationally explain all things in life at the expense of mystery and faith. For example, Scholasticism tried to logically explain how the inner substance of the bread and wine changed to the body and blood of Christ, a belief called transubstantiation. The east accepted that it did change by taking Jesus at His word when He said "This is my body…This is my Blood…"

The concept of Humanism developed during the Renaissance period as the preoccupation with humanity, humanism, and materialism. This detracted from the spiritual aspects of the Church, which is necessary in establishing the faith of each individual. Additionally, religious art deviated to secular themes, as Renaissance art tended to humanize God and Christ, as compared to Byzantine iconography, which emphasizes the divinity of God.

Decline of the Papacy

The supremacy and power of the Pope was fixed by the eleventh century. Large treasuries were required to sustain the extensive land ownership by Rome, and the Pope's involvement in commercial buying and selling and in maintaining large armies. In order to raise the necessary funds needed, the Popes regarded themselves as having the authority to collect significant taxes from all the Christian provinces in the west.

Pope Innocent V in the fifteenth century began selling Church positions, such as bishop's seats, to raise additional income. One example in history shows the Church at one point having a cardinal who was sixteen years of age. As taxes increased, the Church got richer and the Church leaders began to live in excessive wealth and luxury. The Popes also influenced political assignments and appointments of government offices and land titles. With the emergence of new states, nationalism arose. The individual rulers began to question the authority of papal supremacy. As commerce and industry of the individual states expanded, their rulers demanded more and more power. Thus, the emergence of new states, universities, Scholasticism,

Humanism, and Capitalism, along with the decline of the papacy, laid the groundwork for rebellion. Hence the Protestant Reformation, which took place in the sixteenth century.

The Protestant Reformation

There was a time following the Crusades when a conciliatory movement took place in the west. An attempt was made to return to the ancient traditions of the ecumenical councils. The movement advocated a shift from central papal authority to a joint council. However, before the movement could thrive, it died. In spite of this failure, Church officials and layman continued to protest and cry out for reform for the next two centuries.

Two of the early reformers in the Catholic Church were John Wycliffe and John Huss, who stood their ground in the fourteenth and early fifteenth centuries. Determined to see change, John Wycliffe disputed the authority of Rome in intervening in the affairs of the English government and demanding tax assessments from the government. He also disputed the papal system, the hierarchal structure of the Church, and the teaching of the Sacrament of the Holy Eucharist. He emphasized the Bible rather than holy tradition. While Wycliffe pursued various reassessments of Church doctrine, there are some biblical principles that oppose his thinking on the Sacraments, particularly regarding Holy Communion (Last Supper), baptism (Jesus's baptism), ordination (Pentecost), and the wedding where Jesus demonstrated His first miracle.

John Huss, a philosophy professor at the University of Prague, is known for his reaction against the Church regarding the selling of "indulgences." Penances or indulgences in the Western Church were tied into a method of soliciting funds where money given to the treasury of merit would lessen the time spent in purgatory—the intermediate period between death and the Final Judgment. The penances were certified with a paper called indulgences. John Huss was tried by the Church as a heretic, found guilty, and burned at the stake. This practice set the stage for the upcoming Inquisitions.

As Wycliffe and Huss stepped out in faith, following them was the greatest figure in the Protestant Reformation: Martin Luther, a

Dominican monk. Luther was appointed Professor of Philosophy at Wittenberg College at age twenty-five. He was regarded as an authority of Holy Scripture, especially after he translated the Bible from Latin to German. Martin Luther vehemently opposed the practice and sale of indulgences, as well as the force used against Germans to pay for the construction of St. Peter's Church in Rome. These protests directly brought into question papal authority and infallibility. His official protests took the form of his ninety-five theses nailed to the door of the Cathedral in 1513. Luther's movement turned from the traditional teachings of the Church to a theology, which selected only teachings found in the Bible. He only accepted baptism and the Eucharist as Sacraments because he claimed only these are mentioned specifically in the Bible. Luther rejected the traditional teachings of the Church for he believed that faith and good works go hand-in-hand and believed that man could be saved by faith alone. He also believed in predestination, a view where God guides those who are destined for salvation. When Martin Luther was excommunicated by the Church, he organized the Lutheran Church, which opened the door for others to pick and choose what they judged to be valid and true.

John Calvin took the protest movement even further. In 1535, at the age of twenty-six, Calvin wrote what was probably the most influential book of the Protestant Reformation, *The Institutes of the Christian Religion*. Nearly three decades after Calvin's criticism, Queen Elizabeth of England reorganized and took over the authority of the Church of England in 1560. Yet her reign proved to be short-lived when the Pope of Rome later excommunicated her. Out of the Church of England, known as the Anglican Church, sprang up several Protestant churches, including the Congregationalists, Episcopalians, Baptists, Methodists, Presbyterians, Seventh Day Adventists, Mormons, Quakers, Christian Scientists, and Jehovah's Witnesses. In America, most Christians are Protestants, and fallout groups from the Protestants still occur. Today we see TV evangelists and other individuals organizing at will their own congregations, imposing their own beliefs and doctrines. The threat of corruption, however, looms as many of these evangelists accumulate large sums of money using their influence on their congregations.

It has to be pointed out that the deterioration, decline, and divisions that occurred in the Western Church in conjunction with the Protestant Reformation did not take place in the Eastern Church. Church leaders in the east concentrated solely on Church matters and worked hand-in-hand with the government of the Byzantine Empire to remain free from corruption. These same leaders made certain that the doctrines, sacred traditions, and dogmas established by the apostles, and substantiated by the ecumenical councils, were maintained. This practice still continues in the Eastern Orthodox Church of today, regardless of subsequent opposition that took place during the domination of the Ottoman Empire and the Communists while they were in power.

Catholic Church Counter-Reformation Program

The Catholic Church embarked on a reformation program of its own following the Protestant Reformation. This included a three-fold program:

1. Discipline and reform became a must for all clergy.
2. Doctrines and teachings were systemized, defined, and published through catechisms.
   —Clergy were required to obtain a college degree.
3. Church administration and government underwent a complete reorganization. However, Rome continued the status of the power and authority of the Popes by solidifying claims to papal supremacy.

Following the initial reform, several Church councils took place, including the Council of Trent (1545-1563), Vatican I (1870), and Vatican II (1961). The Council of Trent was convened through the initiative of certain political rulers in Germany who wished to put a stop to Protestant Reformation. The French and Spanish bishops who attended wished to reject papal supremacy over all the bishops, and instead the bishops would draw their authority from apostolic succession. They did not succeed. The following is a synopsis of the decisions at the Council of Trent:

- Holy Scriptures and holy tradition are the two sources of divine knowledge and have equal authority, which agrees with Orthodox theology.
- Justification by faith is not enough. It must be augmented with good works. Predestination was rejected. Both tenants are in agreement with Orthodox theology.
- Confirmed Seven Sacraments, which is in agreement with Orthodox theology.
- Pope is Christ's vicar on earth, a doctrine that the Orthodox Church denies.

Vatican Council I convened in 1870. Orthodox and Protestant representatives were invited but did not attend because attendance implied acceptance of papal authority. During this council, papal infallibility was officially adopted. A group of bishops from Germany, Austria, Bohemia, and Switzerland refused to adopt this new policy, claiming that decisions are infallible only when the full body of bishops is in session. This is in agreement with the policy of the Orthodox Church, a belief that still exists in parts of these countries. This group is called "Old Catholics."

In 1961, the Vatican Council reconvened and was called Vatican II. The intent was to ease the tensions and antagonisms between the Catholic Church and the other Christian churches. Unfortunately, little was done to change the differences and disagreements as the papal primacy and infallibility were upheld and conciliatory belief was again rejected. In addition, the problem of the Uniate, or Byzantine Catholic Rite, was not cleared up with the Orthodox Church and still remains a stumbling block between the two churches.

The Roman Catholic Church in America

The first Roman Catholic Church in America was formed in Baltimore in 1634 due to a large influx of immigrants in the mid-1800s and from 1890, especially the Irish and the Italians. The Catholic Church in America is well organized and established. The

Church boasts numerous schools and hospitals throughout the country, and more than 50 million individuals claim membership in the Roman Catholic Church in America.

THE ORTHODOX CHURCH AND THE ECUMENICAL MOVEMENT

In order to assess the role of the Orthodox Church in the Ecumenical Movement, one has to look back to God's original covenants with His chosen people of Israel and to His final covenant with the fullness of time or the coming of Jesus Christ. Since the Jews rejected Christ, the *New Israel, or God's chosen people,* is those who accept Christ and His Church. We have explored how the Orthodox Church has maintained a historical connection with the original Church as established by Christ and His apostles. The patriarchs, prophets, and saints of the Old Testament, along with the apostles, martyrs, and saints of the New Testament, are ever-present living witnesses in the worship and sacrament of the Orthodox Church. Thus, we as Orthodox Christians should believe ourselves to be by virtue of baptism, chrismation, and the Eucharist, along with the other sacraments and beliefs, members of this *One Universal Chosen Nation of God.*

The Emergence and Establishment of the Unified Christian Church

The first indication of ecumenism was after St. Constantine made Christianity legal during the Edict of Milan in 313 AD. From what can be considered a separate nation of Christians during the persecution period of 100-300 AD sprung a multiplicity of peoples that were united religiously, socially, and politically. In addition to the Byzantine Greeks and the Romans, this included the Goths, Huns, Scandinavians, Slavs, Tartars, and Gauls. There was a fusion of culture, heritage, environment, and faith in Jesus Christ, which resulted in one united Christian Church. As new nations and states emerged, the Christian Church developed her dogmas and established forms for worship and policies for administration through both local and ecumenical councils.

Differences Arise

Unfortunately, trials plagued the unified Church, which resulted in the dividing line between the Orthodox Church and the Roman Catholic Church. As history does reveal little chance of reconciliation, it seemed that the One, Holy, Catholic, and Apostolic Church had reached a point that appeared irreversible; there would never come a time when the Christian churches could ever unite again.

A New Spirit of Ecumenism

Reconciliation lingered on the minds of many. After the turn of the twentieth century, the Christian churches, with a renewed spirit, began to have informal meetings, which have evolved today into the Ecumenical Movement. The Ecumenical Patriarch of Constantinople has played a significant role in this movement. In 1902, the ecumenical patriarch issued a Synodical Encyclical addressed to the Patriarchs of Alexandria, Jerusalem, and Antioch, and to the heads of the autocephalous churches. This letter sought to discuss possible harmony. Several years later in 1920, the ecumenical patriarch issued another call to all leaders of Christianity throughout the world, asking them to come to a closer relationship with each other in Christian unity. The encyclical suggested a type of structure be formed that would later lead to dialogue between the churches. Consequently, Faith and Order Meetings were held in Lucerne, Switzerland in 1927 and Edinburgh, England in 1937, and ultimately led to the formation of the World Council of Churches in Amsterdam, Holland in 1948. Since that time, there have been World Council of Church meetings every seven years, and the Orthodox Church has been a participant at each meeting. However, the Roman Catholic Church has not attended any of these meetings. The divide would continue.

A certain degree of Christian unity has been achieved in the twentieth century between Orthodox, Roman Catholics, and Protestants. Unity should not be misconstrued to mean *union* of the different Christian churches. Union presents many stumbling blocks and requires much more than an organization like the World Council of Churches. The Orthodox Church's attitude toward union is to appeal to all churches to return to their tradition, doctrine, ecclesiastical and liturgical worship of the One, Holy, Catholic, and Apostolic Church from which they all came and which does not allow them to remain separate. This calls for all believers to return to the religious, spiritual, and doctrinal attitude of the apostles and the early Church Fathers.

Will Union Ever Be Achieved?

In order to truly achieve union of all Christian churches, one would surmise that it must begin with the two Christian denominations that were responsible for the original schism—that is the Orthodox and the Roman Catholic churches. If this movement were to ever succeed, it would include more than three quarters of the world's Christian population. More importantly, who better to take the first step toward complete Christian unity than those who were involved in the initial schism? Perhaps if this original split had not occurred, the Church would have been strong enough to ward off any attempts to divide the One, Holy, Catholic, and Apostolic Church, such as occurred in the sixteenth and seventeenth centuries with the Protestant movement.

In reviewing the two major splits in the Church—the Great Schism and the Protestant movement—is it possible to determine if there was any one single factor or were their several key factors as the major underlying cause(s) that have left today's one billion-plus Christians split and in disarray? Certainly no one imagines that Christ would want these divisions in His Church as we have today. His command to His disciples to go out and teach the Word of God to both the Jews and the Gentiles throughout the world was meant as one body, one Church.

There is no question that there are dogmatic and doctrinal differences among the three churches. However, the dogmatic differences between the Catholic and Orthodox churches are not great as compared to those differences between the two largest Christian churches and the more than one thousand denominations of the Protestant churches. If the religious differences were the major factors to be resolved in reuniting the Orthodox and Catholic churches, the probability of coming to a consensus over these differences is highly likely. If in fact this is the case, then why hasn't unity occurred over the last one thousand years?

In looking back over this review of Church history, there is one factor that stands out as not only a key reason for the original two divisions but continues to be a major stumbling block in making unification possible today. The Catholic Church is monolithic and operates on the basis of "total authority" and infallibility of the Pope. Its philosophy is to work toward domination of the people through central power and authority of the hierarchy and clergy, including in the individual communities, rather than through direction, instruction, and guidance, and thus relying on the "free will" of the people as given to them by God. The Pope, of course, is the ultimate authority on all matters of the Roman Catholic Church instead of through any form of conciliatory authority.

On the other hand, the Orthodox Christian Church is made up of a group of equal national churches and operates on the basis of Church councils instead of a single dominant central authority such as the Pope. The basic unit in the Church organization is the community, which is operated as a joint effort by the priest and the members of the community. The difference in the philosophies can be clearly seen by attending a mass and a Divine Liturgy. In the Liturgy, the focus is on both the people and the priest so that everyone participates as one body. In contrast, the Catholic mass it seems to focus on the priest while the people are there just to observe. The Orthodox Church believes strongly in *teaching* people the way of God and the Lord Jesus Christ. Each of us then has to accept and follow this way through our free will as given to us by God.

Even today, the Orthodox Church claims willingness to accept the position of the Pope, or Bishop of Rome, as "the first among equals," as it originally was when Rome was the seat of the Roman Empire. However, the Orthodox Church is not willing to accept the present position of the Pope having total authority and being infallible. This would mean that the Orthodox Church would have to relinquish the philosophy of operating on the basis of a conciliatory tradition and forfeit the belief that the community, and thus the people, is the basic unit of the Church. It would also have to operate on the basis of a central authority, which is the Pope, and not through the Holt Synod Church Councils, as it does today. Is this the way our Lord Jesus Christ wanted it? The apostles themselves set a precedent in their first meeting at Jerusalem in 50 AD, when they agreed by *consensus* on several important matters that were instrumental in making the Christian Church a universal Church for both the Jews and the Gentiles.

Two other issues among others that would have to be resolved are the marriage of priests and sexual issues in marriage. The Catholic Church believes that the *only* purpose of sex between a husband and wife is to have children. The stand of the Orthodox Church differs from this in that the Orthodox Church believes that although the *main* purpose of sex between husband and wife is to have children, another major purpose is to promote and strengthen the bonds of love between husband and wife.

Recently Pope Paul stated that he would like to see a union of the Christian churches by the year 2000. However, he followed this call for union by saying that the Catholic Church cannot give up the position of the Pope as Christ's vicar on earth. Did Christ intend that *all His apostles* teach the way of God as He instructed them, or did He intend that the Pope be the sole representative of Christ on earth? It is not likely that the Orthodox Church, and certainly the Protestant denominations, will submit to this unyielding and unrelenting stand by the Catholic Church. This has been an obstacle toward union over the centuries and will continue to be in the future. If the Catholic Church will not move toward a conciliatory approach in Church matters, will the Christian Church ever again be one body as intended by our Lord Jesus Christ?

Chapter 4

CHRONOLOGY OF THE BIBLE READINGS: THE MINISTRY OF CHRIST

The ministry of Christ began on the day He was baptized, the Feast Day of Theophany. The following outlines the major events of His ministry using passages from the Holy Bible, thus recounting teachings of Jesus in the order that the events actually occurred. Knowing the "story" of the ministry of Christ—the major events of His accomplishments in the order that these occurred—gives us a picture of His life by which we can better remember who our Lord is, what He has done, and what the meaning of His ministry is to all of us.

The Bible passages listed below are taken from The Holy Bible New International Version, International Bible Society (14). Any **Church Interpretations** listed are from The Orthodox Study Bible, New Testament, and Psalms, New King James Version, St. Athanasius Orthodox Academy (13).

1. *Jesus Baptized* – *about 26 AD* (**Matt. 3:13-17**); (Mark 1:9-11; (Luke 3:21-23); (John 1:29-39)

Then Jesus came from Galilee to the Jordan to be baptized by John. But John tried to deter Him, saying, "I need to be baptized by You, and do You come to me?" Jesus replied, *"Let it be so now; it is proper for us to do this to fulfill all righteousness."* Then John consented.

As soon as Jesus was baptized, He went up out of the water. At that moment, heaven was opened, and He saw the Spirit of God descending like a dove and lighting on Him. And a voice from heaven said, *"This is my Son, whom I love; with him I am well pleased."*

2. *Jesus Tempted by Satan* – *about 26 AD* (**Matt. 4:1-11**); (Mark 1:12-13); (Luke 4:1-13)

Following His baptism, Jesus was led by the Spirit into the desert to be tempted by the devil. After fasting forty days and forty nights He was hungry. The tempter came to Him and said, "If You are the Son of God, tell these stones to become bread." Jesus answered him, *"It is written, man does not live on bread alone, but on every word that comes from the mouth of God."*

Then the devil took Him to the holy city and had Him stand on the highest point of the temple. "If you are the Son of God" he said, "throw yourself down. For it is written: 'He will command His angels concerning You, and they will lift You up in their hands, so that You will not strike your foot against a stone.'" Jesus answered him, *"It is also written, do not put the Lord your God to the test."*

Again the devil took Him to a very high mountain and showed Him all the kingdoms of the world and their splendor. "All this I will give You," he said, "if You will bow down and worship me." Jesus said to him, *"Away from Me, Satan! For it is written:*
worship the Lord, your God, and serve Him only." Then the devil left Him and angels came and attended

3. *Jesus's First Miracle: Jesus Turns Wine into Water* – *about 26 AD* (**John 2:1-11**)

On the third day a wedding took place at Cana in Galilee. Jesus's mother was there, and Jesus and His followers were also invited to the wedding. When the wine was gone, Jesus's mother said to Him, "They have no more wine." *"Dear woman, why do you involve Me?"*

Jesus replied, *"My time has not yet come."* His mother said to the servants, "Do whatever He tells you."

Nearby stood six stone water jars, the kind used by the Jews for ceremonial washing, each holding from twenty to thirty gallons. Jesus said to the servants, *"Fill the jars with water,"* so they filled them to the brim. Then He told them, *"Now draw some out and take it to the master of the banquet."* They did so and the master of the banquet tasted the water that had been turned into wine. He did not realize where it had come from, though the servants who had drawn the water knew. Then he called the bridegroom aside and said, "Everyone brings out the choice wine first and then the cheaper wine after the guests have had too much to drink, but you have saved the best till now."

This, the first of His miraculous signs, Jesus performed in Cana of Galilee. He thus revealed His glory, and His disciples put their faith in Him. And Jesus went forward to perform many miracles, which the people were awed with.

THE SEVEN SIGNS PERFORMED BY JESUS:

The wedding in Cana is the first of the seven *signs,* or miracles, performed by Jesus as described in the Gospel. These *signs,* as presented in this section, include: changing water into wine (John 2:1–11); curing the nobleman's son (John 4:46–54); healing the paralytic (John 5:1–15); feeding the five thousand (Luke 9:10–19); walking on water (Mark 6:42–56); giving sight to the blind man (John 9:1–12); and raising Lazarus from the dead (John 11:1–44). By His presence at the wedding in Cana, Jesus declares marriage to be holy and honorable, a sentiment supported in Hebrews 13:4, and this passage is read at Orthodox weddings.

4. *Jesus Teaches Nicodemus in Judea – 27 AD:* (John 3:1–21)

Now there was a man of the Pharisees called Nicodemus, a member of the Jewish ruling council. He came to Jesus at night and said, "Rabbi, we know you are a teacher, Who has come from God. For no one could perform the miraculous signs You are doing if God were not with Him." In reply Jesus declared, *"I tell you the truth, no one can enter the kingdom of God, unless he is born again."* "How can a man be born when he is old?" Nicodemus asked. "Surely he cannot enter his mother's womb a second time to be born!" Jesus answered, *"I tell you the truth, no one can enter the kingdom of God unless he is born of water and spirit. Flesh gives birth to flesh, but the Spirit gives birth to spirit. You should not be surprised at my saying. You must be born again. The wind blows whenever it pleases. You hear its sound, but you cannot tell where it comes from or where it is going. So it is with everyone born of the spirit."* "How can that be?" Nicodemus asked. *"You are Israel's teacher,"* said Jesus, *"and do you not understand these things? I tell you the truth, we speak of what we know, and we testify to what we have seen, but still you people do not accept our testimony. I have spoken to you of earthly things and you do not believe; how then will you believe if I speak of heavenly things? No one has ever gone into heaven except the one who came from heaven – the Son of Man. Just as Moses lifted up the snake in the desert, so the Son of Man must be lifted up, that everyone who believes in Him may have eternal life. For God so loved the world that He gave His one and only Son, that whoever believes in Him shall not perish but have eternal life. For God did not send His Son into the world to condemn the world, but to save the world through Him. Whoever believes in Him is not condemned, but whoever does not believe stands condemned already because he has not believed in the name of God's one and only Son. This is the verdict: Light has come into the world, but men loved darkness instead of light because their deeds were evil. Everyone who does evil hates the light, and will not come into the light for fear that his deeds will be exposed. But whoever lives by the truth comes into the light, so that it may be seen plainly that what he has done has been done through God."*

5. ***The First Four Disciples – 27 AD*** **(Luke 8:1–11);** (Matt. 4:18–22); (Mark 1:16–20)

So it was, as the multitude pressed about Him to hear the word of God that He stood by the Lake of Gennesaret and saw two boats standing by the lake, but the fishermen had gone from them and were washing their nets. Then He got into one of the boats, which was Simon's, and asked him to put out a little from the land. And He sat down and taught the multitude from the boat. When He had stopped speaking, He said to Simon and his brother Andrew, *"Launch out into the deep and let down your nets for a catch."* But Simon answered and said to Him, "Master, we have toiled all night and caught nothing; nevertheless at your word I will let down the net." And when they had done this, they caught a great number of fish, and their nets were breaking. So they signaled to their partners in the other boat to come and help them. And they came and filled both the boats, so they began to sink.

When Simon Peter saw it, he fell down at Jesus's knees, saying, "Depart from me, for I am a sinful man, O Lord!" For he and all that were with him were astonished at the catch of fish, which they had taken; and so also were James and John, the sons of Zebedee, who were partners with Simon. And Jesus said to them, *"Do not be afraid. From now on you will catch men."* So when they had brought their boats to land, they forsook all and followed Him.

6. *Jesus Talks to The Samaritan Woman* – 27 AD; **(John 4:5–42)**

The Pharisees heard that Jesus was gaining and baptizing more disciples than John, although in fact it was not Jesus who baptized, but His disciples. When the Lord learned of this, He left Judea and went back once more to Galilee.

Now He had to go through Samaria. So He came to a town in Samaria called Sychar, near the plot of ground Jacob had given to his son Joseph. Jacob's well was there, and Jesus, tired as He was from the journey, sat down by the well. It was about the sixth hour. when a Samaritan woman came to draw water, Jesus said to her, *"Will you give me a drink."* (His disciples had gone into the town to buy food.) The Samaritan woman said to Him, "You are a Jew and I am a Samaritan woman. How can you ask me for a drink?" (For Jews don't associate with Samaritans.) Jesus answered her, *"If you knew the gift of God and Who it is that asks you for a drink, you would have asked*

Him and he would have given you living water." "Sir," the woman said, "you have nothing to draw with and the well is deep. Where can you get this living water? Are you greater than our father Jacob, who gave us the well and drank from it himself, as did also his sons and his flocks and herds?" Jesus answered, *"Everyone who drinks this water will be thirsty again, but whoever drinks the water I give him will never thirst. Indeed the water I give him will become in him spring of water welling up to eternal life."* The woman said to Him, "Sir give me this water so that I won't get thirsty and have to keep coming here to draw water." He told her, *"Go call your husband and come back."* "I have no husband." She replied. Jesus said to her, *"You are right when you say you have no husband. The fact is, you have had five husbands, and the man you have now is not your husband. What you have just said is quite true."* "Sir," the woman said, "I can see that you are a prophet. Our fathers worshiped on this mountain, but you Jews claim that the place that we must worship is in Jerusalem." Jesus declared. *"Believe me, woman, the time is coming you will worship the Father neither up this mountain nor in Jerusalem. You Samaritans worship what you do not know; we worship what we do know, for salvation is from the Jews. Yet a time is coming and has now come when the true worshipers will worship the Father in spirit and truth, for they are the kind of worshipers the Father seeks. God is spirit and His worshipers must worship in spirit and in truth."* The woman said, "I know that Messiah (called Christ) is coming. When he comes, he will explain everything to us." Then Jesus declared, *"I who speak to you am he."*

Just then the disciples returned and were surprised to find Him talking with a woman

But no on asked, "What do you want?" or "Why are you talking with her?"

Then leaving her water jar, the woman went back to the town and said to the people, "Come see a man who told me everything I ever did. Could this be the Christ?" They came out of town and made their way toward Him.

Meanwhile, His disciples urged Him, "Rabbi eat something." But He said to them, *"I have food to eat that you know nothing about."* Then His disciples said to each other, "Could someone have brought

Him food?" *"My food,"* said Jesus, *"is to do the will of Him Who sent me and to finish His work. Do you not say, 'Four months more and then the harvest?' I tell you, open your eyes and look at the fields! They are ripe for harvest. Even now the reaper draws his wages, even now he harvests the crop for eternal life, so that the sower and the reaper may be glad together. Thus the saying, 'One sows and another reaps' is true. I sent you to reap what you have not worked for. Others have done the hard work and you have reaped the benefits of their labor."*

Many of the Samaritans from the town believed in Him because of the woman's testimony, "He told me everything I ever did." So, when the Samaritans came to Him, they urged Him to stay with them, and He stayed two days. And because of His words many more became believers. They said to the woman, "We no longer believe just because of what you said; now we have heard for ourselves, and we know that this man is the Savior of the world."

7. *Jesus Heals a Nobleman's Son – 27 AD* (John 4:46–54)

Once more Jesus visited Cana in Galilee, where He had turned the water into wine. And there was a certain royal official whose son lay sick in Capernaum. When this man heard that Jesus had arrived in Galilee from Judea, he sent to Him and begged Him to heal his son, who was close to death. *"Unless you people see miraculous signs and wonders,"* Jesus told him, *"you will never believe."* The royal official said, "Sir, come down before my child dies." Jesus replied, *"You may go. Your son will live."*

The man took Jesus at His word, and departed. While he was still on his way, his servants met him with the good news that his boy was living. When he inquired as to the time when his son got better, they said to him, "The fever left him yesterday at the seventh hour." Then the father realized that this was the exact time at which Jesus had said to him, "Your son will live." So he and his entire household believed. This was the second miraculous sign that Jesus had performed, having come from Judea to Galilee.

8. *Jesus Heals the Paralytic – 27 AD* (John 5:1–15)

After this there was a feast of the Jews, and Jesus went up to Jerusalem. Now there is in Jerusalem by the sheep gate a pool, which is called in Hebrew, Bethseda, having five porches. In these lay a great multitude of sick people, blind, lame, paralyzed, waiting for the moving of the water. For an angel went down at a certain time into the pool and stirred up the water; then whoever stepped in first, after the stirring of the water, was made well of whatever disease he had.

Now a certain man was there who had an infirmity thirty-eight years. When Jesus saw him lying there, and knew that he already had been in that condition a long time, He said to him, *"Do you want to be made well?"* The sick man answered Him, "Sir, I have no man to put me into the pool when the water is stirred up, but while I am coming, another steps down before me." Jesus said to him, *"Rise take up your bed and walk."* And immediately the man was made well, took up his bed, and walked. And that day was the Sabbath.

The Jews therefore said to him who was cured, "It is the Sabbath; it is not lawful for you to carry your bed." He answered them, *"He who made me well said to me, 'Take up your bed and walk.'"* Then they asked him, "Who is the man who said to you, *'Take up your bed and walk?'"* But the one who was healed did not know who it was, for Jews had withdrawn, a multitude being in that place.

Afterward Jesus found him in the temple, and said to him, *"See, you have been made well, Sin no more, lest a worse thing come upon you."* The man departed and told the Jews that it was Jesus who had made him well.

9. *Jesus Heals Peter's Mother-in-law and Many Others* – 27 AD; **(Mark 1:29–34)**; (Matt. 8:14–17); (Luke 4:38–41)

As soon as they left the synagogue, they went with James and John to the home of Simon and Andrew. Simon's mother-in-law was in bed with a fever, and they told Jesus about her. So He went to her, took her hand and helped her up. The fever left her and she began to wait on them.

That evening after sunset the people brought to Jesus all the sick and demon-possessed. The whole town gathered at the door, and Jesus healed many who had various diseases. He also drove off many demons, but He would not let the demons speak because they knew who He was.

10. *Jesus Begins His First Preaching and Healing Trip through Galilee* – *27 AD;* **(Matt. 4:23–25);** (Mark 1:35–39);(Luke 4:42–44)

Jesus went throughout Galilee, teaching in their synagogues, preaching the good news of the kingdom, and healing every disease and sickness among the people.

News about Him spread all over Syria, and people brought to Him all who were ill with various diseases, those suffering severe pain, the demon-possessed, those having seizures, and the paralyzed, and He healed them. Large crowds from Galilee, Jerusalem, Judea and the region across the Jordan followed Him.

11. *Jesus Chooses His Twelve Disciples to Go Out to Preach and Heal* – *28 AD;* **(Mark 3:13–19);** (Luke 6:12–15)

Jesus went up on a mountainside and called to Him those He wanted, and they came to Him. He appointed twelve—designating them apostles—that they might be with Him and that He might send them out to preach and to have authority to drive out demons. These are the twelve that He appointed: Simon (to whom He gave the name Peter); James son of Zebedee and his brother John (to them He gave the name Boanerge, which means "sons of thunder"); Andrew, Philip, Bartholomew, Matthew, Thomas, James son of Alphaeus, Thaddeus, Simon the Zealot and Judas Iscariot, who betrayed Him.

12. *Jesus Preaches the Sermon on the Mount* – *28 AD* **(Matt. 5:1–7:29)**; (Luke 6:20–49)

The actual Bible passages for the Sermon on the Mount are not included in this segment. Rather, discussed here are the Church interpretations of the Scriptures, which include four primary themes offered by Jesus in His Sermon on The Mount. These four elements are: *The Beatitudes; The New Covenant; Spiritual Disciplines; Exhortations to Righteousness.* The topics related to each theme are also included. These Church interpretations are extracted from The Orthodox Study Bible (13), Matthew 5:1 through 7:29. After reading through the explanations below, it is recommended that this passage from Matthew be carefully read for further enlightenment.

In the Sermon on the Mount, Jesus introduces the kind of life those who seek the Kingdom of God must lead. His homily could properly be called, "Righteousness for the Kingdom."

(1) The Beatitudes (Matt. 5:1–16): The sermon begins with the Beatitudes (the "blessings"), describing the joys of true discipleship the blessed way of life. The people of God await the rewards of the promises Jesus makes. The actual Bible passages with the corresponding Church interpretations for the Beatitudes are included in Chapter 8 "Reading The Holy Bible," pp 116–119.

(2) The New Covenant (Matt. 5:17–48): Then, as the Son of God, whose authority is greater than Moses's, Christ proclaims the new law, the righteous leading toward perfection, to which the Mosaic Law and the Old Testament prophets pointed. Jesus reveals the deeper meaning of several Old Testament laws, broadening their implications.

(a) "You shall not murder" is expanded beyond the command against physically killing another person (Matt. 5:21–26). Murder now implies anger, calling someone a fool and degrading him, or failure to be reconciled with a friend or adversary.

(b) "You shall not commit adultery" no longer refers merely to the unlawful act of sex outside of marriage. It now includes lust (Matt. 5:27).

(c) Divorce was allowable under the Old Testament law, but under the New Covenant, divorce is only permissible due to sexual immorality; remarriage to a divorced person is not permitted (Matt. 5:31,32).

(d) "Perform your oaths to the Lord" is an Old Testament law. Jesus instructs us to say "yes" or "no" without taking an oath, and to simply keep our word (Matt. 5:33–37).

(e) "An eye for an eye" is a graphic way of seeing justice from a human perspective, yet it now becomes "turn the other cheek" and "love your enemies." Not only must we forsake vengeance, even when it is founded in retribution, but we must treat others as God treats us, with mercy and grace (Matt. 6:1–4).

(3) *Spiritual Disciplines* (Matt. 6:1–7:12): Jesus assumes we will follow three disciplines, that help us attain true righteousness (Matt. 6:1–18) and true wisdom (Matt. 6:19–7:12). These disciplines are a vital part of Christian tradition.

(a) Giving alms, or doing charitable deeds for the poor, should be done secretly, before God, not before men (Matt. 6:1–4).

(b) Prayer should follow the model of the Lord's Prayer, which Jesus here reveals to His Church (Matt. 6:5–15).

(c) Fasting should likewise be done for God, not for men (Matt. 6:16–18)

These spiritual disciplines help us find true wisdom, which consists of: (1) the love of God and pursuit of His righteousness by bringing our treasure (Matt. 6:19– 26) as alms to God, and our worries (Matt. 6:22–7:34) in prayer, and fasting to Him; and (2) the love of human beings and pursuit of righteous reconciliation with them by submitting our judgments of them (Matt. 7:1–6) to God's severe mercy. For these difficult tasks we need divine discernment and guidance, which God provides to those who follow Jesus's spiritual rule (Matt. 7:7–12). Thus our natural impulses are redirected toward their proper goal—the righteousness of God in His kingdoms (Matt. 6:33).

(4) Exhortations in Righteousness (Matt. 7:13–29): Jesus concludes with exhortations to true righteousness, warnings about hypocritical and deceitful professions of righteousness, and instructions to build on the rock of His teachings.

13. *Jesus Tells Parables About His Kingdom* – 28 AD
(**Luke 8:4–15**); (Matt. 13:1–52); (Mark 4:1–34)

Parable of the Sower:

And when a great multitude had gathered, and they had come to Him from every city, He spoke by a parable:

"A sower went out to sow his seed. And as he sowed, some fell by the wayside; and it was trampled down and the birds of the air devoured it." "Some fell on the rock; and as soon as it sprang up, it withered away because it lacked moisture." "And some fell among thorns, and the thorns sprang up with it and choked it." "But others fell on good ground, sprang up, and yielded a crop a hundredfold." When He had said these things He cried out, *"He who has ears to hear, let him hear!"* Then His disciples asked Him, saying, "What does this parable mean?" And He said, *"To you it has been given to know the mysteries of the kingdom of God, but to the rest it is given in parables, that 'Seeing they may not see, and hearing they may not understand.'" "Now the parable is this: The seed is the word of God. Those by the wayside are the ones who hear; then the devil comes and takes away the word out of their hearts, lest they should believe and be saved. But the ones on the rock are those, who when they hear, receive the word of God with joy; and these have no root, who believe for awhile and in time of temptation fall away. Now the ones that fell among thorns are those who when they have heard, go out and are choked with cares, riches, and pleasures of life, and bring no fruit to maturity. But the ones that fell on the good ground are those who, having heard the word with a noble and good heart, keep it and bear fruit with patience."*

What Are Parables?

Parables are stories using word-pictures, to reveal spiritual truths. The Scriptures, especially the gospels, are filled with parables—images drawn from daily life in the world that represent and communicate the depths of God's love. Parables give us glimpses of Him whose thoughts are not our thoughts and whose ways are not our ways.

Parables challenge the hearer and call for faith to perceive the mysteries of the kingdom. They offer insight into God's Kingdom and speak of God Himself through vivid stories. His purpose was not only to reveal truth to those with hearts prepared. He also wished to draw responsive hearts past the entrance and into the very reality of God's Kingdom, which Jesus proclaimed and inaugurated.

In opening up to us the door to the Kingdom of Heaven, the parables help us to love God and to know Him, to understand and believe His grace, mercy and forgiveness, and order our lives according to His Holy Word.

Parables also fulfill prophecy (Matt. 13:34, 35): All these things Jesus spoke to the multitude in parables; and without a parable He did not speak to them, that it might be fulfilled which was spoken by the prophet saying; *"I will open my mouth in parables; I will utter things kept secret from the foundation of the world."*

In addition to the Parable of the Sower, among other familiar parables that Jesus spoke throughout His ministry—and that are read on Sunday throughout the church year are: the Good Samaritan (Luke 10:25–37); the Rich Man and His Crops (Luke 12:16–21); The Great Supper (Luke 14:16–24); the Talents (Matt. 25:14–30); the Pharisee, the Tax Collector (Luke 18:10–14); and the Prodigal Son (Luke 15:11–32).

14. *Jesus Quiets the Storm on the Sea of Galilee* – *28 AD* **(Mark 4: 35–41)**; (Matt. 8:23–27); (Luke 8:22–25)

On the same day, when evening had come, He said to them, *"Let us cross to the other side."* Now when they had left the multitude, they took Him along in the boat as He was. And other little boats were also with Him. And a great windstorm arose, and the waves beat into the boat, so that it was already filling. But He was in the stern asleep on a pillow. And they awoke Him and said to Him, "Teacher, do you not care that we are perishing?" Then He arose and rebuked the wind, and said to the sea, *"Peace be still."*

And the wind ceased and there was a great calm. But He said to them, *"Why are you so fearful? How is it that you have no faith?"* And they feared exceedingly, and said to one another, "Who can this be, that even the wind and the sea obey Him!"

15. *Jesus Sends His Twelve Followers Out to Preach and Heal* – *28 AD* (**Mark 6:6–13**); (Matt. 9:35–11:1); (Luke 9:1–6)

And He called the twelve to Himself, and began to send them out two by two, and gave them power over unclean spirits. He commanded them to take nothing for the journey except a staff—no bags, no bread, no copper in their money belts—but to wear sandals, and not to put on two tunics.

And He said to them, *"In whatever place you enter a house, stay there till you depart from that place. And whoever will not receive you, when you depart from there, shake off the dust under your feet as a testimony against them. Assuredly, I say to you, it will be more tolerable for Sodom and Gomorrah in the day of judgment than for that city!"*

So they went out and preached that people should repent. And they cast out many demons, and anointed with oil many who were sick, and healed them.

16. *Jesus Feeds the Five Thousand* – *Spring 29 AD* (**Luke 9:10–17**); (Matt. 14:13–21); (Mark 6:30–44); (John 6:1–14)

When the apostles returned, they reported to Jesus what they had done. Then He took them with Him and they withdrew by themselves to a solitary place near Bethsaida, but the crowds learned about it and followed Him. He welcomed them and spoke to them about the kingdom of God, and healed those who needed healing.

Late in the afternoon the Twelve came to Him and said, "Send the crowd away so they can go to the surrounding villages and countryside and find food and lodging, because we are in a remote place here. He replied, *"You give them something to eat."* They answered, "We have only five loaves of bread and two fish—unless we go out and buy food for all this crowd." (About five thousand men were there.) But He said to his disciples, *"Have them sit down in groups of about fifty each."*

The disciples did so, and everybody sat down. Taking the five loaves and the two fish and looking up to heaven, He gave thanks and broke them. Then He gave them to the disciples to set before the people. They all ate and were satisfied, and the disciples picked up twelve baskets of broken pieces that were left over.

17. *Jesus Walks on Water and Heals the Sick* – *Spring 29 AD* (**Mark 6:42–56**); (Matt.14:22–36)

Immediately Jesus made His disciples get into the boat and go on ahead of Him to Bethsaida, while He dismissed the crowd. After leaving them, He went up on a mountainside to pray.

When evening came, the boat was in the middle of the lake, and He was alone on land. He saw the disciples straining at the oars, because the wind was against them. About the fourth watch of the night He went out to them, walking on the lake. He was about to pass by them, but when they saw Him walking on the lake, they thought He was a ghost. They cried out, because they all saw Him and were terrified. Immediately He spoke to them and said, *"Take courage! It is I. Do not be afraid."* Then He climbed into the boat with them, and the wind died down. They were completely amazed, for they had not understood about the loaves to the five thousand; their hearts were hardened.

When they had crossed over, they landed at Gennesaret and anchored there. As soon as they got out of the boat, people recognized Jesus. They ran throughout the whole region and carried the sick on mats to wherever they heard He was. And wherever He went—into villages, towns, or countryside—they placed the sick in the marketplaces. They begged Him to let them touch even the edge of his cloak, and all who touched Him were healed.

18. **Peter Says that Jesus Is the Son of God** – *Later 29 AD*
    (Matt. 16:13–20); (Mark 8:1–9)

When Jesus came to the region of Caesarea Philippi, He asked His disciples, *"Who do people say the Son of Man is?"* They replied, " Some say John the Baptist, others say Elijah; and still others, Jeremiah or one of the prophets." *"But what about you?"* He asked, *"Who do you say I am?"* Simon Peter answered, "You are the Christ, the Son of the living God."

Jesus replied, *"Blessed are you Simon son of Jonah, for this was not revealed to you by man, but by my Father in heaven. And I tell you that you are Peter, and on this rock I will build my church, and the gates of Hades will not overcome it. I will give you the keys of the kingdom of heaven; whatever you bind on earth will be bound in heaven, and whatever you loose on earth will be loosed in heaven."* Then He warned His disciples not to tell anyone He was Christ.

19. **Jesus Predicts His Death** – *Later29 AD* **(Mark 8:31–37);** (Matt. 16:21–26); (Luke 9:22–23)

He then began to teach them that the Son of Man must suffer many things and be rejected by the elders, chief priests, and teachers of the law, and that He must be killed and after three days rise again. He spoke plainly about this, and Peter took Him aside and began to rebuke Him. But when Jesus turned and looked at His disciples, He rebuked Peter. *"Get behind Me, Satan!"* He said. *"You do not have in mind the things of God, but the things of men."*

Then He called the crowd to Him, along with His disciples, and said: *"If anyone would come after Me, he must deny himself and take up his cross and follow Me. For whoever wants to save his life will lose it, but whoever loses his life for Me and for the gospel will save it. What good is it for a man to gain the whole world yet forfeit his soul? Or what can a man give in exchange for his soul?"*

20. **The** *Transfiguration of Jesus* – *Later 29 AD* **(Matt. 17:1–13);** (Mark 9:2–13); (Luke 9:28–36)

After six days Jesus took with Him Peter, James and John the brother of James, and led them up a high mountain by themselves. There He was transfigured before them. His face shown like the sun, and His clothes became as white as the light. Just then there appeared before them Moses and Elijah, talking with Jesus.

Peter said to Jesus, "Lord, it is good for us to be here. If you wish, I will put up three shelters—one for You, one for Moses, and one for Elijah."

While he was still speaking, a bright cloud enveloped them, and a voice from the cloud said, *"This is my Son, whom I love; with Him I am well pleased. Listen to Him!"*

When the disciples heard this, they fell face down to the ground, terrified. But Jesus came and touched them. *"Get up."* He said. *"Don't be afraid."* When they looked up, they saw no one except Jesus. As they were coming down the mountain, Jesus instructed them. *"Don't tell anyone what you have seen, until the Son of Man is raised from the dead."*

The disciples asked Him, "Why then do the teachers of the law say that Elijah must come first?" Jesus replied, *"To be sure, Elijah comes and will restore all things. But I tell you, Elijah has already come, and they did not recognize him, but have done to him everything they wished. In the same way the Son of Man is going to suffer at their hands."* Then the disciples understood that He was talking to them about John the Baptist.

21. *Jesus at the Feast of Tabernacles* – *October 29 AD* (John 7:11–46)

When the Jewish Feast of the Tabernacles was near, Jesus's brothers said to Him, "You ought to leave here and go to Judea, so that your disciples may see the miracles you do." Now at the Feast the Jews were watching for Him and asking, "Where is that man?" Some said, "He is a good man," and others said "No, He deceives the people."

Not until halfway through the Feast did Jesus go up to the temple courts and begin to teach. The Jews were amazed and asked, "How did this man get such learning without having studied?" Jesus answered,

"My teaching is not my own. It comes from Him, who sent me. If anyone chooses to do God's will, he will find out whether my teaching comes from God or whether I speak on my own. He who speaks on his own does so to gain honor for himself, but he who works for the honor of the One who sent him is a man of truth; there is nothing false about him. Has not Moses given you the law? Yet not one of you keep the law. Why are you trying to kill me?" "You are demon-possessed," the crowd answered. "Who is trying to kill you?" Jesus said to them, *"I do one miracle and you all are astonished. Yet because Moses gave you circumcision, you circumcise a child on the Sabbath. Now if a child can be circumcised on the Sabbath so that the law of Moses may not be broken, why are you angry with Me for healing a whole man on the Sabbath? Stop judging by mere appearances, and make a right judgment."*

At that point, some of the people of Jerusalem began to ask, "Isn't this the man our leaders are trying to kill? Here He is speaking publicly, and they are not saying a word

to Him. Have the authorities really concluded that He is the Christ? But we know where this man is from; when the Christ comes, no one will know where he is from." Then Jesus still teaching in the temple courts cried out, *"Yes you know me, and you know where I am from. I am not here on my own, but He who sent me is true. You do not know Him. But I know Him because I am from Him and He sent me."* At this point, they tried to seize Him, but no one laid a hand on Him, because his time had not yet come. The Pharisees heard the crowd murmuring these things concerning Him, and the Pharisees and chief priests sent officers to take Him.

Still, many in the crowd put their faith in Him. They said, "When the Christ comes, will he do more miraculous signs than this man?" Jesus said, *"I am with you for only a short time, and then I go to the one who sent me. You will look for me, but you will not find me; and where I am, you cannot come."* The Jews said to one another, "Where does this man intend to go so that we cannot find Him?"

On the last and greatest day of the Feast, Jesus stood and said in a loud voice, *"If anyone is thirsty, let him come to Me and drink. Whoever believes in Me, as the Scripture has said, streams of living water will flow from within him."* By this He meant the Spirit, whom those who believe in Him were later to receive. Up to that time the Spirit had not been given, since Jesus had not yet been glorified. On hearing His words, some of the people said, "Surely this man is the prophet." Others said, "He is the Christ." Still others asked, "How can the Christ come from Galilee? Does not the Scripture say that the Christ will come from David's family and from Bethlehem, the town where David lived?" Thus the people were divided because of Jesus. Some wanted to seize Him, but no one laid a hand on Him.

Finally the temple guards went back to the chief priests and Pharisees, who asked them, "Why didn't you bring Him in?" The guards declared, "No one ever spoke the way this man does."

22. *Jesus Does Not Condemn the Adulterous Woman –* *October 29 AD* (**John 8:1–11**)

Then at night each went to his own home. But Jesus went to the Mount of Olives. At dawn, He appeared again in the temple courts, where all the people gathered around Him, and He sat down to teach them. The teachers of the law and the Pharisees brought in a woman caught in adultery. They made her stand before the group and said to Jesus, "Teacher, this woman was caught in the act of adultery. In the Law, Moses commanded us to stone such women. Now what do you say?" They were using this question as a trap, in order to have a basis for accusing Him.

But Jesus bent down and started to write on the ground with His finger. When they kept on questioning Him, He straightened up and said to them, *"If anyone of you is without sin, let him be the first to throw a stone at her."* Again He stooped down and wrote on the ground.

At this, those who heard began to go away one at a time, the older ones first, until only Jesus was left, with the woman still standing there. Jesus straightened up and asked her, *"Woman, where are they? Has no one condemned you?"* "No one, sir." she said. *"Then neither do I condemn you,"* Jesus declared, *"Go now and leave your life of sin."*

23. *Jesus Heals a Man Who Was Born Blind* – *October 29 AD* (John 9:1–12)

As Jesus left the temple grounds, He saw a blind man from birth. His disciples asked Him, "Rabbi, who sinned, this man or his parents, that he was born blind?" *"Neither this man nor his parents sinned,"* said Jesus, *"but this happened that the work of God might be displayed in his life. As long as it is day, we must do the work of Him who sent Me. Night is coming, when no one can work. While I am in the world, I am the light of the world."* Having said this, He spit on the ground, made some mud with the saliva, and put it on the man's eyes. *"Go,"* He told him, *"wash in the pool of Siloam."* So the man went and washed, and came home seeing.

His neighbors and those who had formerly seen him begging asked, "Isn't this the same man who used to sit and beg?" Some claimed that he was. Others said, "No, he only looks like him." But he himself insisted, "I am the man." "How then were your eyes opened?" they demanded. He replied, "The man they call Jesus made some mud and put it on my eyes. He told me to go to Siloam and wash. So I went and washed, and then I could see." "Where is this man," they asked him. "I don't know," he said.

24. *Jesus Raises Lazarus from the Dead* – *Late 29 AD* (John 11:1–44)

Now a man named Lazarus was sick. He was from Bethany, the village of Mary and her sister Martha. This Mary, whose brother Lazarus now lay sick, was the same one who would pour perfume on the Lord and wipe His feet with her hair. So the sister sent word to Jesus. "Lord, the one You love is sick." When He heard this, Jesus said, *"This sickness will not end in death. No, it is for God's glory so that God's Son may be glorified through it."* Jesus loved Martha and her sister and Lazarus. Yet when He heard that Lazarus was sick, He stayed where He was two more days.

Then He said to his disciples, *"Let us go back to Judea."* "But Rabbi," they said, "a short while ago the Jews tried to stone You, and yet You are going back there?" Jesus answered, *"Our friend Lazarus has fallen asleep, but I am going there to wake him up."*

On His arrival, Jesus found that Lazarus had already been in the tomb for four days. Bethany was less than two miles from Jerusalem, and many Jews had come to Martha and Mary to comfort them in the loss of their brother. When Martha heard that Jesus was coming, she went out to greet Him, but Mary stayed home. "Lord," Martha said to Jesus, "If You had been here my brother would not have died. But I know that even now, God will give You whatever You ask." Jesus said to her, *"Your brother will rise again."* Martha answered, "I know he will rise again in the resurrection of the last day." Jesus said to her, *"I am the resurrection and the life. He who believes in Me will live, even though he dies; and whoever lives and believes in Me will never die. Do you believe this?"* "Yes Lord," she told Him, "I believe that You are the Christ, the Son of God, Who was to come into the world."

And after she had said this, she went back and called her sister Mary aside. "The Teacher is here," she said, "and is asking for you." When Mary heard this, she got up quickly and went to Him. When Mary reached the place where Jesus was and saw Him, she fell at His feet and said, "Lord, if You had been here my brother would not have died." When Jesus saw her weeping, and the Jews who had come along with her also weeping, He was deeply moved in spirit and was troubled. *"Where have you laid him?"* He asked. "Come and see Lord," they replied.

Jesus, once more deeply moved came to the tomb. It was a cave with a stone laid across the entrance. *"Take away the stone,"* He said. "But Lord," said Martha, "by this time there is a bad odor, for he has been there four days." Then Jesus said, *"Did I not tell you that if you believed, you would see the Glory of God?"* So they took away the stone. Then Jesus looked up and said, *"Father, I thank You that You have heard Me. I knew that You always hear Me, but I said this for the benefit of the people standing here, that they may believe that You sent Me."* When He had said this, Jesus called in a loud voice, *"Lazarus, come out!"* The dead man came out, his hands and feet wrapped with strips of linen, and a cloth around his face. Jesus said to them, *"Take off the grave clothes and let him go."*

25. *Jesus Begins His Last Trip to Jerusalem and Cleanses Ten Lepers* – *30 AD* (Luke 17:11–19)

Now it happened as He went to Jerusalem that He passed through the midst of Samaria and Galilee. Then as He entered a certain village, there met Him ten men who were lepers who stood afar off. And they lifted up their voices and said, "Jesus, Master, have mercy on us!" So when He saw them, He said to them, *"Go, show yourselves to the priests."* And so it was as they went, they were cleansed.

And one of them, when he saw that he was healed, returned, and with a loud voice glorified God, and fell down on his face at His feet, giving Him thanks. And he was a Samaritan.

So Jesus answered and said, *"Were there not ten cleansed? But where are the nine? Were there not any found who returned to give glory to God except this foreigner?"*

And He said to him, *"Arise go your way. Your faith has made you well."*

26. *Children Receive the Kingdom with Jesus's Blessing* – *30 AD* (Mark 10:13–16); (Matt.19: 13–15); (Luke 18:15–17)

Then they brought little children to Him, that He might touch them, but the disciples
rebuked those who brought them. But when Jesus saw it, He was greatly displeased and said to them, *"Let the little children come to Me, and do not forbid them; for of such is the kingdom of God. Assuredly I say to you, whoever does not receive the kingdom of God as a little child will by no means enter it."* And He took them up in His arms, laid His hands on them, and blessed them.

27. *Jesus Again Tells About His Death and Resurrection – 30 AD* **(Luke 18:31–34);** (Matt. 20:17–19); (Mark 10:32–34)

Then He took the twelve aside and said to them, *"Behold, we are going up to Jerusalem, and all things that are written by the prophets concerning the Son of Man will be accomplished. For, He will be delivered to the Gentiles and will be mocked and insulted and spit upon. They will scourge Him and kill Him. And the third day He will rise again."* But they understood none of these things; this saying was hidden from them, and they did not know the things, which were spoken.

THE LAST WEEK – 30 AD:

28. *Jesus's Triumphal Entry into Jerusalem – Sunday* **(Mark 11:1–10);** (Matt. 21:1–11); (Luke 19:29–44); (John 12:12–19)

As theapproached Jerusalem and came to Bethphage and Bethany at the Mount of Olives, Jesus sent two of His disciples saying to them, *"Go to the village ahead of you, and just as you enter it, you will find a colt tied there, which no one has ever ridden. Untie it and bring it here. If anyone asks you, 'Why are you doing this?' tell him, 'The Lord needs it and will bring it back shortly.'"*

They went and found a colt outside in the street, tied at a doorway. As they untied it, some people standing there asked, "What are you doing, untying that colt?" They answered as Jesus told them to and the people let them go. When they brought the colt to Jesus and threw their cloaks over it, He sat on it. Many people spread their cloaks on the road, while others spread branches and palms they had cut in the fields. Those who went ahead and those who followed shouted:

"Hosanna!"

"Blessed is He who comes in the name of the Lord!"

"Blessed is the coming kingdom of our father David!"

"Hosanna in the highest!"

Jesus entered Jerusalem and went to the temple. He looked around at everything, but since it was already late, He went out to Bethany with the twelve.

29. *Jesus Cleanses the Temple* – *Monday* (**Mark 11:15–18**); (Matt. 21:12,13); (Luke 19:45–48)

On reaching Jerusalem, Jesus entered the temple area, and began driving out those who were buying and selling there. He overturned the tables of the moneychangers and the benches of those selling doves, and would not allow anyone to carry merchandise through the temple courts. And as He taught them, He said, *"Is it not written: 'My house will be called a house of prayer for all nations?' But you have made it a den of robbers."* The chief priests and the teachers of the law heard this and began looking for a way to kill Him, for they feared Him, because the whole crowd was amazed at His teaching.

30. *The Authority of Jesus Questioned* – *Tuesday* (**Mark 11:27–33**); (Matt. 21:23–27); (Luke 20:1–8)

They arrived again in Jerusalem, and while Jesus was teaching the gospel to the people in the temple courts, the chief priests, the elders of the law, and the elders came to Him. "By what authority are you doing these things?" they asked. "And who gave you authority to do this?" Jesus replied, *"I will ask you one question. Answer Me and I will tell you by what authority I am doing these things. John's baptism—was it from heaven, or from men? Tell me!"* They discussed it among themselves and said, "If we say 'From heaven, He will ask, "Then why didn't you believe him?' But if we say, 'From men'"—(They feared the people, for everyone held that John really was a prophet). So they answered Jesus, "We don't know." Jesus said, *"Neither will I tell you by what authority I am doing these things."*

31. *Jesus Teaches in The Temple* – *Tuesday* (**Luke 20:9–21:4**); (Matt. 21:28–23:39); (Mark 12:1–44)

The Parable of the Tenants:

He went on to tell the people this parable: *"A man planted a vineyard, rented it to some farmers, and went away for a long time. At harvest time he sent a servant to the tenants so they would give him some of the fruit of the vineyard. But the tenants beat and sent him away empty-handed. He sent another servant, but that one also they beat and treated shamefully and sent away empty-handed. He sent still a third, and they wounded him and threw him out.*

Then the owner of the vineyard said, 'What shall I do? I will send my son, whom I love; perhaps they will respect him.' But when the tenants saw him, they talked the matter over. 'This is the heir,' they said. 'Let's kill him, and the inheritance will be ours.' So they threw him out of the vineyard and killed him. What then will the owner of the vineyard do to them? He will come and kill those tenants and give the vineyard to others." When the people heard this, they said, "May this never be!" Jesus looked directly at them and asked, *"Then what is the meaning of that which is written: 'The stone the builders rejected has become the chief cornerstone.' Whoever falls on that stone will be broken to pieces, but he on whom it falls will be crushed."*

The Scribes—the teachers of the law—and the chief priests looked for a way to arrest Him immediately, because they knew He had spoken this parable against them. But they were afraid of the people.

Church Interpretation: This parable recounts the history of Israel. God the Father is the owner. The vineyard is Israel. The tenants are the religious leaders. The servants are the prophets. The beloved son is Jesus the Messiah. The others are the Gentiles. The quotation about the *chief cornerstone* refers to Christ, the foundation stone rejected by the religious leaders, and who becomes *chief cornerstone* of the Church.

Paying Taxes to Caesar:

Keeping a close watch on Him, the religious leaders sent spies, who pretended to be honest. They hoped to catch Jesus in something He said so that they might hand Him over to the power and authority of the governor. So the spies questioned Him: "Teacher, we know that You speak and teach what is right, and that You do not show partiality, but teach the way of God in accordance with the truth. Is it right for us to pay taxes to Caesar, or not?"

Jesus saw through their craftiness and said to them, *"Show me a denarius. Whose portrait and inscription are on it?"* "Caesar's." they replied. He said to them, *"Then give to Caesar what is Caesar's, and to God what is God's."* They were unable to trap

Him in what He had said there in public. And astonished by His answer, they became silent.

Church Interpretation: The question on Roman taxation is designed to trap Jesus between loyalty to the Roman government and to the Jewish people. A "yes" would turn the people against Him. A "no" would bring a charge of treason by the Roman governor. His answer defeats their cunning, and shows that no conflict need exist between civic and religious duties. Christians can render the state while serving God. As the coin bears the image of the emperor and is properly paid to him, so each person bears the image of God and belongs to Him. Conflict arises when the state demands of Christians what belongs to God.

The Resurrection and Marriage:

Some of the Sadducees, who say there is no resurrection, came to Jesus with a question. "Teacher," they said, "Moses wrote for us that if a man's brother dies and leaves a wife but no children, the man must marry the widow and have children for his brother. Now there were seven brothers. The first one married a woman and died childless. The second and then the third married her, and in the same way the seven died, leaving no children. Finally, the woman died too. Now then, at the resurrection whose wife will she be, since the seven were married to her?"

Jesus replied, *"The people of this age marry and are given in marriage. But those who are considered worthy of taking part in the age and in the resurrection from the dead will neither marry nor be given in marriage, and they can no longer die; for they are with the angels.*

They are God's children, since they are children of the resurrection. But in the account of the bush, even Moses showed that the dead rise, for he calls the Lord 'The God of Abraham, and the God of Isaac, and the God of Jacob.' He is not the God of the dead, but of the living, for to Him all are alive." Some of the teachers of the law responded, "Well said Teacher!" And no one dared to ask Him any more questions.

Church Interpretation: The Sadducees were the high priestly and landowning class, which controlled the temple and the Jewish Council. In a striking difference with the Pharisees, the Sadducees rejected the resurrection of the dead and they came to Christ to dispute it. Jesus's answer is concise and irrefutable. Since, *God is not the God of the dead bur of the living,* both those who are physically alive and those who are deceased, such as Abraham, Isaac, and Jacob, *all live in Him.*

Whose Son Is the Christ:

Then Jesus said to them, *"How is it that they say the Christ is the Son of David? David himself declares in the Book of Psalms: 'The Lord said to my Lord; "Sit at my right until I make your enemies a footstool for your feet.' David calls Him 'Lord.' How then can He be His son?"*

Church Interpretation: The first reference to *Lord* in the Book of Psalms applies to God the Father, the second reference to *Lord* is to Christ whom David, the writer of this Psalm, calls *my Lord.* The riddle has its solution in that the Messiah is David's Son in His humanity, yet David calls Him *Lord* in His eternal deity.

Beware of the Scribes:

While all the people were listening, Jesus said to His disciples, *"Beware of the teachers of the law. They like to walk around in flowing robes and love to be greeted in the marketplace and have the most important seats in the synagogues and the places of honor at the banquets. They devour widows' houses and for a show make lengthy prayers. These will receive greater condemnation."*

The Widow's Offering:

As He looked up, Jesus saw the rich putting their gifts into the temple treasury. He also saw a widow put in two very small copper coins. *"I tell you the truth,"* He said, *"this poor widow has put in more than all the others. All these people gave their gifts out of their wealth, but she out of her poverty put in all she had to live on."*

32. *The Plot Against Jesus – Tuesday* (**Matt. 26:1–5**)

When Jesus had finished preaching all these things at the temple, He said to His disciples, *"As you know the Passover is two days away—and the Son of Man will be handed over to be crucified."*

Then the chief priests and the elders of the people assembled in the palace of the high priest, whose name was Caiaphas, and they plotted to arrest Jesus in some sly way and kill Him. "But not during the Feast," they said, "or there may be a riot among the people."

33. *Jesus Anointed at Bethany – Tuesday* (**Luke 12:2–11**); (Matt. 26:6–13); (Mark 14:3–9)

Jesus arrived at Bethany, where Lazarus lived, whom Jesus had raised from the dead. Here a dinner was given in Jesus's honor. Martha served, while Lazarus was reclining at the table with Him. Then Mary took about a pint of pure nard, an expensive perfume; she poured it on Jesus's feet and wiped His feet with her hair. And the house was filled with the fragrance of the perfume.

But one of His disciples, Judas Iscariot, who was later to betray Him, objected, "Why wasn't this perfume sold and the money given to the poor? It was worth a year's wages." He did not say this because he cared about the poor but because he was a thief; as keeper of the moneybag, he used to help himself to what was put into it. *"Leave her alone,"* Jesus replied. *"It was intended that she should save this perfume for the day of my burial. You will always have the poor among you, but you will not always have Me."*

Meanwhile a large crowd of Jews found out that Jesus was there and came, not only because of Him, but also to see Lazarus, whom

He had raised from the dead. So the chief priests made plans to kill Lazarus as well, for on account of him many of the Jews were going over to Jesus and putting their faith in Him.

34. *Judas Iscariot Plots to Betray Jesus* – *Wednesday* (Matt. 26:14–16); (Mark 14:10, 11); (Luke 22:3–6)

Then one of the twelve—the one called Judas Iscariot—went to the chief priests and asked, "What are you willing to give me if I hand him over to you?" So they counted out for him thirty silver coins. From then on Judas watched for an opportunity to hand Him over.

35. *The Last Supper* – *Thursday* (Matt. 26:17–30); (Mark 14:2–25); (Luke 22:7–20) (John 13:1–36)

On the first day of the Feast of Unleavened Bread, the disciples came to Jesus and asked, "Where do you want us to make preparations for You to eat the Passover?" He replied, *"Go into the city to a certain man and tell him, 'The Teacher says: My appointed time is near. I am going to celebrate the Passover with My disciples at your house.'"* So the disciples did as Jesus directed them and prepared the Passover.

When evening came, Jesus was reclining at the table with the Twelve. And while they were eating, He said, *"I tell you the truth, one of you will betray Me."* They were very sad and began to say to Him, one after the other, "Surely not I, Lord?" Jesus replied, *"The one who has dipped his hand into the bowl with Me will betray Me. The Son of Man will go just as it is written about Him. But woe to that man who betrays the Son of Man! It would be better for him if he had not been born."*

Then Judas, the one who would betray Him, said, "Surely not I, Rabbi?" Jesus answered, *"Yes, it is you."*

While they were eating, Jesus took bread, gave thanks and broke it, and gave it to His disciples, saying *"Take and eat, this is my body."*

Then He took the cup, gave thanks and offered it to them, saying, *"Drink of it all of you. This is My blood of the covenant, which is poured out for many for the forgiveness of sins. I tell you, I will not drink of this fruit of the vine from now on until the day when*

I drink it anew with you in My Father's Kingdom." After they sung a hymn, they went out into the Mount of Olives.

36. Peter's Denial Foretold – *Thursday* (John 13:36–38); (Matthew 26:31–35); (Mark 14:27–31); (Luke 22:31–34)

Simon Peter said to Him, "Lord, where are You going?" Jesus answered him, *"Where I am going you cannot follow me now, but you shall follow Me afterward."*

Peter said to Him, "Lord why can I not follow You now? I will lay down my life for Your sake."

Jesus answered him, *"Will you lay down your life for My sake? Most assuredly, I say to you, the rooster shall not crow till you have denied Me three times."*

37. *Jesus Preaches to and Gives Comfort to The Disciples* – *Thursday* (John 13:34; 14:1–16:33

Jesus went out from the Last Supper in the middle of the night and preached and gave comfort to His disciples.

The New Commandment:

"A new commandment I give you, that you love one another; as I loved you."

Church Interpretation: What is new about Christ's commandment? In the Law of Moses, the command was "to love your neighbor as yourself." In Christ's command, we love one another *"as I have loved you."* This means that Christ's love for us is the true measure for how we are to love our neighbor.

The Way to the Father:

Jesus said, *"I am the way, the truth, and the life. No one comes to the Father except through Me If you had known Me, you would have known My Father also; and from now on you know Him and have seen Him."*

Church Interpretation: *"The way, the truth, and the life"* is a Person, our Lord Jesus Christ. He is the ultimate truth because of His perfect union with His Father. *The way* we reach the Father is forever established through the Son. Jesus is the *truth* because He is the unique revelation of the Father, who is the goal of our journey through life. Christ is *the life,* the uncreated eternal life manifests in the flesh, so that we may have life. Because of this, n*o one comes to the Father except through the Son.* While aspects of goodness and truth are found among all people by virtue of their being created in the image and likeness of God, *salvation comes through Christ alone.*

The Coming of the Holy Spirit:

"And I will pray the Father, and He will give you another Helper, that He may abide with you forever the Spirit of truth, whom the world cannot receive, because it neither sees Him nor knows Him; but you know Him, for He dwells with you and will be in you."

Church Interpretation: The apostles did not fully understand the teachings and works of Christ prior to the reception of the Holy Spirit on Pentecost. Jesus calls us to know *the Spirit of truth* who is in us and helps us pray. Thus prayer in Jesus's name relates to all three Persons of the Holy Trinity *the Father, the Son, and the Holy Spirit.* Jesus gives assurance that such prayer is answered for those who are united with Him.

The Son's Presence and Departure:

"A little while longer and the world will see Me no more, but you will see Me. Because I live, you will live also. At that day you will know that I am in My Father, and you in Me, and I in you. He who has My commandments and keeps them, it is he who loves Me. And he who

loves Me, will be loved by My Father, and I will love him and manifest myself to him. He who has My commandments and keeps them, it is he who loves Me. And he who loves Me will be loved by My Father, and I will love him and manifest Myself in him."

Church Interpretation: The brief separation of Jesus from the disciples, due to His arrest and Crucifixion, will lead to a deeper mystical union after the Resurrection and the gift of the Holy Spirit at Pentecost. *At that day* refers to the Resurrection of Jesus followed by the ascension and the giving of the Holy Spirit at Pentecost, all of which, working together, make the fullness of divine life available to all believers. With the sending of *the Helper, the Holy Spirit, whom the Father will send in My name,* we have confidence in the apostles' doctrine (Acts 2:42) because the Holy Spirit is their Teacher and brings Christ's words to their remembrance. We have confidences in the Church, the guardian of the faith, because of our teacher, the Holy Spirit.

Union and Communion With Christ:

"I am the true vine, and My Father is the vinedresser. Abide in Me, and I in you. As the branch cannot bear fruit of itself, unless it abides in the vine, neither can you, unless you abide in Me."

Church Interpretation: The vine is a symbol of Israel. In contrast to disobedient and unfruitful Israel, Jesus calls Himself *the true vine,* which, together with its branches, constitutes a new and fruitful people of God, the Church. Abiding in Christ is living out our union with Him in faith, baptism, love, obedience, and the Eucharist. The figure of the vine and branches shows: (1) our union with Christ is intimate and real we are a new people in Christ; (2) life flows from the vine to the branches abiding in Christ is not static nor "positional," but dynamic and vitalizing; and (3) the fruit we bear is both good works and mission. Those who do not abide in Christ bear no fruit, and are cut off from Him.

Keeping Christ's Commandments:

"If you keep My commandments, you will abide in My love, just as I have kept My Father's commandments and abide in His love. These things I have spoken to you, that My joy may remain in you, and that your joy may be full."

Church Interpretation: The fact is, God does love us unconditionally, no matter what our response may be. But His unconditional love does us no good unless we keep His commandments and abide in His love. We show our love for God by obeying Him wholeheartedly.

"This is My commandment, that you love one another as I have loved you. Greater love has no one than this, than to lay down one's life for his friends. You are My friends if you do whatever I command you. No longer do I call you servants, for a servant does not know what his master is doing; but I have called you friends, for all things that I heard from My Father I have made known to you."

Church Interpretation: Just as God loves us unconditionally, so we are to love each other unconditionally in Christ's name—whether there is a response or not. Friendship is higher than servanthood. A servant obeys his master out of fear; a friend is a servant who obeys out of love. Abraham was called a "friend of God" (James 2:23) because he believed and obeyed God. The disciples and the saints are honored as friends of Christ and heirs of God in Romans 8:17: "and if children then heirs, heirs of God and joint heirs with Christ." Here Jesus tells his *friends* those things He has heard from His Father, the truths and blessings, which He reveals in this gospel.

The World's Hatred:

"If the world hates you, you know that it hated Me before it hated you. Remember the word that I said to you, 'A servant is not greater than his master.' If they persecuted Me, they will persecute you. But all these things they will do to you for My name's sake, because they do not know Him who sent Me. If I had not come and spoken to them, they would have no sin, but now they have no excuse for their sin. He who hates Me,

hates My Father also. But when the helper comes, whom I shall send to you from the Father, the Spirit of Truth who proceeds from the Father, He will testify of Me."

Church Interpretation: Regarding the world we learn that: (1) while union with Christ brings love, joy, and peace, it also reaps the world's hatred and persecution; (2) the citizens of the world who hate Christians do so because they do not know the Father; (3) a person cannot say that he loves God but not God's Son, for those who hate Christ also hate God the Father; and (4) hatred for Jesus Christ is without legitimate cause, for He brings God's love and truth to the world.

With respect to God's work in the world, the Son will *send the Spirit .from the Father.* With respect to His divinity, the Spirit originates or *proceeds from the Father* alone. The Spirit receives His eternal existence only from the Father. In conformity with Christ's words, the Nicene Creed confesses belief "in the Holy Spirit, the Lord and giver of life, who proceeds from the Father." By contrast, the Son is eternally begotten of the Father. The source, the fountainhead, of both is the Father.

The Work of the Holy Spirit:

"Nevertheless I tell you the truth. It is to your advantage that I go away; for if I do not go away, the Helper will not come to you; but if I depart, I will send Him to you. And when He has come, He will convict the world of sin, and of righteousness, and of judgment: of sin, because they do not believe in Me; of righteousness, because I go to My Father and you will not see Me no more; of judgment, because the ruler of this world is judged."

"However, when He the Spirit of truth, has come; He will guide you into the truth; for He will not speak on His own authority, but whatever He hears He will speak and He will tell you things to come."

Church Interpretation: Through the illumination of the Holy Spirit, the world will be convicted, that is, proved wrong and judged about: (1) *sin* – the ultimate sin is not to believe in Jesus as God and man, crucified and resurrected; (2) *righteousness* – a right relationship with God, possible only through Christ, who is risen, ascended, and righteous before God; (3) *judgment* – all who reject Christ, and are under the sway of the devil, will be given the same penalty their ruler has already received. Because the Church is given this promise of being guided into all truth, she trusts the work of the Spirit on behalf of those who have gone before her: holy tradition.

Death, Resurrection, *and* Ascension Foretold:

"A little while, and you will not see Me; and again a little while and you will see Me, because I go to the Father." Then some of His disciples said among themselves, "What is this He says to us?" Now Jesus knew that they desired to ask Him, and He said to them, *"Are you inquiring among yourselves about what I said, 'A little while, and you will not see Me; and again a little while, and you will see Me?' Most assuredly, I say to you that you will weep and lament, but the world will rejoice; and you will be sorrowful, but your sorrow will be turned into joy."*

"These things I have spoken to you, that in Me, you may have peace. In the world you will have tribulation; but be of good cheer, I have overcome the world."

Church Interpretation: The first little while is the period of the arrest, death, and burial of Jesus; the second little while is the time He is in the tomb. Joy will come with the revelation of Christ risen from the dead, after the sorrow of the cross. Yet Jesus does not promise that sorrow will be removed. His promise is that no one can remove our joy.

Despite persecution and suffering, Christians can maintain the peace and joy of Jesus Christ who has *overcome the world* of darkness through His saving work.

38. *Gethsemane* – *Thursday* (**Matt. 26:36–46**); (Mark 14:32–42); (Luke 22:40–46)

Then Jesus went with His disciples to a place called Gethsemane, and He said to them, *"Sit here while I go over there and pray."* He took Peter and the two sons of Zebedee (James and John) along with Him, and He began to be sorrowful and troubled. Then, He said to them, *"My soul is overwhelmed with sorrow to the point of death. Stay here and keep watch with Me."*

Going a little farther, He fell with His face to the ground and prayed, *"My Father, if it is possible, may the cup be taken from Me. Yet not as I will, but as You will."*

Then He returned to His disciples and found them sleeping. *"Could you men not keep watch with Me for one hour?"* he asked Peter. *"Watch and pray so that you will not fall into temptation. The spirit is willing, but the body is weak."*

He went away a second time and prayed, *"My Father, if it is not possible for the cup to be taken away unless I drink it, may Your will be done."*

When He came back, He again found them sleeping because their eyes were heavy. So He left them and went away once more and prayed the third time, saying the same thing. Then He returned to the disciples and said to them, *"Are you still sleeping and resting? Look the hour is near, and the Son of Man is betrayed into the hands of sinners. Rise, let us go! Here comes my betrayer!"*

39. *Jesus's Arrest and Trial* – Thursday/Friday (**Mark 14:43–15:15**); (Matt. 26:47–27:26); (Luke 22:47–23:25); (John 18:2–19:16)

Jesus Arrested:

Just as He was speaking, Judas, one of the Twelve, appeared. With him were a crowd armed with swords and clubs, sent from the chief priests, the teachers of the law, and the elders. Now the betrayer had arranged a signal with them: "The one I kiss is the man; arrest him and lead him away under guard." Going at once to Jesus, Judas said, "Rabbi!" and kissed Him. The men seized Jesus and arrested Him. Then one of those standing near drew his sword and struck the servant of the high priest, cutting off his ear. *"Am I leading a rebellion,"* said Jesus, *"that you have come out with swords and clubs to capture me? Every day I was with you, teaching in the temple courts and you did not capture me. But the scriptures must be fulfilled."* At that time, everyone deserted Him and fled.

Before the Sanhedrin:

They took Jesus to the high priests; and all the chief priests, elders, and teachers of the law came together. Peter followed Him at a distance, right into the courtyard of the high priest. There he sat with the guards and warmed himself at the fire.

The chief priests and the whole Sanhedrin were looking for evidence against Jesus so that they could put Him to death, but they did not find any. Many testified against Him, but their statements did not agree. Then some stood up and gave this false testimony against Him: "We heard Him say, 'I will destroy this man-made temple and in three days will build another, not made by man.'" Yet even then their testimony did not agree. Then the high priest stood up before them and asked Jesus, "Are you not going to answer? What is this testimony that these men are bringing against You?" But Jesus remained silent and gave no answer. Again the high priest asked Him, "Are You the Christ, the Son of the Blessed One?" *"I am," said Jesus. "And you will see the Son of Man sitting at the right hand of the Mighty One and coming on the clouds of heaven."* The high priest tore His clothes. "Why do we need anymore witnesses?" he asked. "You have heard the blasphemy. What do you think?"

They all condemned Him as worthy of death. Then some began to spit at Him; they blindfolded Him, struck Him with their fists, and said, "Prophecy!" And the guards took Him and beat Him.

Peter Disclaims Jesus:

While Peter was below in the courtyard, one of the servant girls of the high priest came by. When she saw Peter warming himself, she looked closely at him. "You also were with that Nazarene, Jesus," she said. But he denied it. "I don't know or understand what you are talking about," he said, and went out into the entryway. When the servant girl saw him there, she said again to those standing around, "This fellow is one of them." Again he denied it.

After a little while, those standing near said to Peter, "Surely you are one of them for you are a Galilean." He began to call down curses on himself, and he swore to them, "I don't know this man you're talking about." Immediately the rooster crowed the second time. Then Peter remembered the word that Jesus had spoken to him: "Before the rooster crows twice you will deny me three times." And he broke down and wept.

Judas Hangs Himself:

Early in the morning, all the chief priests and the elders of the people came to the decision to put Jesus to death. They bound Him, led Him away and handed Him over to Pilate, the governor.

When Judas, who had betrayed Him, saw that Jesus was condemned, he was seized with remorse and returned the thirty silver coins to the chief priests and the elders. "I have sinned," he said, "for I have betrayed innocent blood." "What is this to us?" they replied. "That's your responsibility." So Judas threw the money into the temple and left. Then he went away and hanged himself.

The chief priests picked up the coins and said, "It is against the law to put this into the treasury, since it is blood money." So they decided to use the money to buy the potter's field as a burial place for foreigners. This is why it has been called the Field of Blood to this day. Then what was spoken by Jeremiah the prophet was fulfilled: "They took the thirty silver coins, the price set on him by the people of Israel, and they used them to buy the potter's field, as the Lord commanded me."

Jesus Before Pilate:

Meanwhile Jesus stood before the governor, and the governor asked Him, "Are you the king of the Jews?" *"Yes, it is as you say,"* Jesus replied. The chief priests accused Him of many things. So again Pilate asked Him, "Aren't You going to answer? See how many things they are accusing You of." But Jesus still made no reply, and Pilate was amazed.

Now it was the custom of the Feast to release a prisoner whom the people requested. A man called Barabbas was imprisoned with the insurrectionists, who had committed murder in the uprising. The crowd came up and asked Pilate to do for them what he usually did. "Do you want for me to release to you the king of the Jews?" asked Pilate, knowing it was out of envy that the chief priests had handed Jesus over to him. But the chief priests stirred up the crowd to have Pilate release Barabbas instead. "What shall I do then with the one you call the king of the Jews?" Pilate asked them. "Crucify Him!" they shouted. "Why? What crime has He committed?" asked Pilate. But they shouted all the louder. "Crucify Him!" Wanting to satisfy the crowd, Pilate released Barabbas to them. He had Jesus flogged and handed Him over to be crucified.

The Soldiers Mock Jesus:

The soldiers led Jesus away into the palace (that is the Praetorium) and called together the whole company of soldiers. They put a purple robe on Him, then twisted together a crown of thorns and set it on Him. And they began to call out to Him, "Hail, king of the Jews!" Again and again they struck Him on the head with a staff and spit on Him. Falling on their knees they pretended to pay homage to Him. And when they had mocked Him, they took off the purple robe and put His own clothes on Him. Then they led Him out to crucify Him.

40. *Jesus's Crucifixion and Death* – *Friday* (Luke 23:26–49); (Matt. 27:27–56); (Mark 15:16–41); (John 19:17–30)

As the soldiers led Him away, they seized Simon from Cyrene, who was on his way in from the country, and put the cross on him and made him carry it behind Jesus. A large number of people followed Him, including women who mourned and wailed for Him. Jesus turned and said to them, *"Daughters of Jerusalem, do not weep for me; weep for yourselves and for your children. For the time will come when you will say, 'Blessed are the barren women, the wombs that never bore and the breasts that never nursed!'"*

Two other men, both criminals, were also led out with Him to be executed. When they came to the place called Golgotha (the skull), there they crucified Him, along with the criminals one on His right, the other on His left. Jesus cried, *"Father, forgive them for they do not know what they are doing."* And they divided up His clothes by casting lots. The people stood watching and the rulers even sneered at Him. "He saved others; let Him save himself if He is the Christ of God, the Chosen One." The soldiers also came up and mocked Him. They offered Him wine vinegar and said, "If you are the king of the Jews, save yourself." There was a written notice above Him, which read, THIS IS THE KING OF THE JEWS.

One of the criminals, who hung there, hurled insults at Him. "Aren't you the Christ? Save yourself and us!" But the other criminal rebuked him. "Don't you fear God," he said, "since you are under the same sentence? We are punished justly, for we are getting what our deeds deserve. But this man has done nothing wrong." Then he said, "Jesus remember me when You come into your kingdom." Jesus answered him, *"I tell you the truth, today you will be with me in paradise."*

Near the cross of Jesus stood his mother, His mother's sister, Mary the wife of Clopas, and Mary Magdalene. When Jesus saw his mother there, and the disciple whom He loved (John) standing nearby, He said to his mother, *"Dear woman, here is your son,"* and to the disciple, *"Here is your mother."* And from that time on, this disciple took her into his home.

At the sixth hour, darkness came over the whole land until the ninth hour. And in the ninth hour Jesus cried out in a loud voice, *"Eloi, Eloi, lama sabach-thani?"*—which means, *"My God, My God, why have You forsaken Me?"* When some of those standing near heard this, they said, "Listen, He's calling Elijah." One man ran, filled a sponge, put it on a stick, and offered it to Jesus to drink. "Now leave Him alone. Let's see if Elijah comes to take Him down." He said.

With a loud cry, Jesus breathed His last and gave up His spirit. At that moment, the curtain of the temple was torn in two, from top to bottom. The earth shook and the rocks split. The tombs broke open and the bodies of many holy people who had died were raised to life. They came out of the tombs and after Jesus's resurrection they went into the holy city and appeared to many people. When the centurion and those with him who were guarding Jesus saw the earthquake and all that had happened, they were terrified, and exclaimed, "Surely He was the Son of God!"

Some other women were watching from a distance. Among these were Mary the mother of James the younger and of Joses, and Salome. In Galilee, these women had followed Him and cared for His needs. Many other women who had come up with Him to Jerusalem were also there.

41. *The Burial of Jesus* – *Friday/Saturday* (Matt. 27:57–66); (Mark 15:42–47); (Luke 23:50–56); (John 19:31–42)

As evening approached, there came a rich man from Arimathea, named Joseph, who had, himself, became a disciple of Jesus. Going to Pilate, he asked for Jesus's body, and Pilate ordered that it be given to him. Joseph took His body, wrapped in a clean linen cloth, and placed it in his own new tomb that he had cut out of the rock. He rolled a big stone in front of the entrance to the tomb and went away. Mary Magdalene and the other Mary, and the other women who had come with Him from Galilee were sitting there opposite the tomb. They observed the tomb and how His body was laid. Then they returned and prepared spices and fragrant oils. And they rested on the Sabbath according to the commandment.

On the Sabbath, the day after Preparation Day, the chief priests and the Pharisees went to Pilate. "Sir," they said, "we remember that while He was still alive that deceiver said, 'After three days I will rise again.' So give the order for the tomb to be made secure until the third day. Otherwise, His disciples may come and steal the body and tell the

people that He has been raised from the dead. This last deception will be worse than the first." "Take a guard," Pilate answered. "Go make the tomb as secure as you know how." So they went and made the tomb secure by putting a seal on the stone and posting the guard.

AFTER THE RESURRECTION – 30 AD:

42. *The Resurrection and the Empty Tomb* – *Sunday*
(**John 20:1–9**); (Matt. 28:1–10); (Mark 16:1–8); (Luke
24:1–12)

Early on the first day of the week, while it was still dark, Mary
Magdalene went to the tomb and saw that the stone had been
removed from the entrance. So she came running to Simon Peter
and the other disciple, the one Jesus loved, and said, "They have
taken the Lord out of the tomb, and we don't know where they have
put Him!"

So Peter and the other disciple started for the tomb. Both were
running, but the other disciple outran Peter and reached the tomb
first. He bent over and looked in at the strips of linen lying there
but did not go in. Then Simon Peter, who was behind him, arrived
and went into the tomb. He saw the strips of linen lying there, as
well as the burial cloth that had been around Jesus's head. The cloth
was folded up by itself, separate from the linen. Finally the other
disciple, who had reached the tomb first, also went inside. He saw
and believed.

43. *The Risen Christ Appears* – *Sunday* (**John 20:10–18**);
(Mark 16:9–13)

Then the disciples went back to their homes, but Mary Magdalene
stood outside the tomb crying. As she wept, she bent over to look
into the tomb and saw two angels in white seated where Jesus's body
had been, one at the head and the other at the foot. They asked her,
"Women, why are you crying?" "They have taken my Lord away,"
she said, "and I don't know where they have put Him." At this, she
turned around and saw Jesus standing there, but she did not realize
that it was Jesus. *"Woman"*, He said, *"why are you crying? Who is it
you are looking for?"* Thinking he was the gardener, she said "Sir, if
you have carried Him away, tell me where you have put Him, and
I will get Him." Jesus said to her, *"Mary."* She turned toward Him
and cried out in Aramaic, "Rabboni!" (which means Teacher). Jesus

said, *"Do not hold on to Me, for I have not yet returned to My Father. Go instead to my brothers and tell them, 'I am returning to My Father and your Father, to My God and your God.'"* Mary Magdalene went to the disciples with the news: "I have seen the Lord!" And she told them that He had said these things to her. When the disciples heard this that Jesus was alive and that she had seen Him, they did not believe her.

Afterward Jesus appeared in a different form to two of them while they were walking on the road to Emmaus. These returned and reported it to the rest; but they did not believe them either.

44. *Jesus Appears to Ten Disciples* – *Sunday* (**John 20:19–25**); (Luke 24:36–43)

On the evening of the first day of the week, when the disciples were together, with the doors locked for fear of the Jews, Jesus came and stood among them and said, *"Peace be with you!"* After He said this, He showed them his hands and side. The disciples were overjoyed when they saw the Lord. Again Jesus said, *"Peace be with you! As the Father has sent Me, I am sending you."* And with that He breathed on them and said, *"Receive the Holy Spirit. If you forgive anyone his sins, they are forgiven; if you do not forgive them, they are not forgiven."*

Now Thomas, one of the twelve, was not with the disciples when Jesus came. So the other disciples told him, "We have seen the Lord!" But he said to them, "Unless I see the nail marks in His hands, and put my finger where the nails were, and put my hand into His side, I will not believe it."

45. *Jesus Appears to the Eleven Disciples* – *One Week Later* (**John 20:26–33**)

A week later His disciples were in the house again, and Thomas was with them. Though the doors were locked, Jesus came and stood among them and said, *"Peace be with you!"* Then He said to Thomas, *"Put your finger here; see my hands. Reach out your hand and put it into my side. Stop doubting and believe."* Thomas said,

"My Lord and my God!" Then Jesus told him, *"Because you have seen Me, you have believed; blessed are those who have not seen and yet have believed."* Jesus did many other miraculous signs in the presence of His disciples, which are not recorded in this book. But these are written that you may believe that Jesus is the Christ, the Son of God, and that by believing you may have life in His name.

46. *Jesus Talks Again with Some of His Disciples* – (John 21:1–25)

Afterward Jesus appeared again to His disciples by the Sea of Tiberias. It happened this way: Simon Peter, Thomas, Nathanael from Cana in Galilee, and two other disciples were together. "I'm going to fish," Simon Peter told them; they said, "We'll go with you." So they went out and got into the boat, but that night they caught nothing.

Early in the morning, Jesus stood on the shore, but the disciples did not realize it was Jesus. He called out to them, *"Friends, haven't you any fish?"* "No!" they answered. He said, *"Throw your net on the right side of the boat and you will find some."* When they did, they were unable to haul the net in because of the large number of fish. Then the disciple whom Jesus loved said to Peter, "It is the Lord!" As soon as Simon Peter heard him say, "It is the Lord," he wrapped his outer garment around himself (for he had taken it off) and jumped into the water. The other disciples followed in the boat, towing the net full of fish, for they were not far from the shore, about a hundred yards. When they landed, they saw a fire of burning coals there with fish on it, and some bread.

Jesus said to them, *"Bring some of the fish you have just caught."* Simon Peter climbed aboard and dragged the net ashore. It was full of large fish, 153, but even with so many the net was not torn. Jesus said to them, *"Come and have breakfast."* None of the disciples dared ask Him, "Who are you?" They knew it was the Lord. Jesus came, took the bread and gave it to them, and did the same with the fish. This was now the third time Jesus appeared to His disciples after He was raised from the dead.

When they had finished eating, Jesus said to Simon Peter, *"Simon, son of John, do you truly love Me more than these?"* "Yes, Lord," he said, "You know that I love You." Jesus said, *"Take care of my sheep."* The third time He said to him*, "Simon son of John, do you love Me?"* Peter was hurt because Jesus asked him the third time, *"Do you love me?"* He said, "Lord, You know all things; You know that I love You." Jesus said, *"Feed my sheep. I tell you the truth, when you were younger, you dressed yourself and went where you wanted; but when you are old you will stretch out your hands, and someone else will dress you and lead you where you do not want to go."* Jesus said this to indicate the kind of death by which Peter would glorify God. Then He said to him, *"Follow me!"*

Peter turned and saw that the disciple whom Jesus loved was following them. (This was the one who had leaned back against Jesus at the supper and had said, "Lord, who is going to betray You?") When Peter saw him, he asked, "Lord, what about him?" Jesus answered, *"If I want him to remain alive until I return, what is that to you? You must follow Me."* Because of this, the rumors spread among the brothers that this disciple would not die. But Jesus did not say that he would not die; He only said, *"If I want him to remain alive until I return, what is that to you?"*

This is the disciple who testifies to these things and who wrote them down. We know this testimony is true. Jesus did many other things as well. If every one of them were written down, I suppose that even the whole world would not have room for the books that would be written.

(Note: The disciple John was the only one not killed and martyred, but died a natural death about 100 AD. As Jesus instructed, the Virgin Mary lived with John while she was alive.)

47. *The Ascension: Jesus Returns to His Father in Heaven*
(40 Days Later) – **(Acts 1:2–26)**

Days 1–39 – Jesus's Promise of the Holy Spirit:

It was previously written about all that Jesus began to do and to teach until the day that He was taken up to heaven, after giving instructions through the Holy Spirit to the apostles He had chosen. After His suffering, He showed Himself to these men and gave many convincing proofs that He was alive. He appeared to them over a period of forty days and spoke about the Kingdom of God. On one occasion while He was eating with them, He gave them this command: *"Do not leave Jerusalem, but wait for the gift my Father promised, which you have heard Me speak about. For John baptized with water, but in a few days you will be baptized with the Holy Spirit."*

So when they met together, they asked Him, "Lord, are You at this time going to restore the kingdom to Israel?" He said to them, *"It is not for you to know the time or dates the Father has set by His own authority. But you will receive power when the Holy Spirit comes to you; and you will be My witnesses in Jerusalem, and in all Judea and Samaria, and to the ends of the earth."*

Day 40– The Ascension:

After He said this, He was taken up before their very eyes, and a cloud hid Him from their sight. They were looking up intently up into the sky as He was going, when suddenly two men dressed in white stood beside them. "Men of Galilee," they said, "why do you stand here looking into the sky? This same Jesus, who has been taken from you into heaven, will come back in the same way you have seen Him go into heaven."

Day 40–49 – Preparation for Pentecost:

Then they returned to Jerusalem from the hill called the Mount of Olives, a Sabbath day's walk from the city. When they arrived, they went upstairs to the room where they were staying. Those present were: Peter, John, James and Andrew; Philip and Thomas, Bartholomew and Matthew; James son of Alphaeus and Simon the Zealot, and Judas son of James. They all joined together constantly in prayer, along with the women and Mary the mother of Jesus, and with His brothers.

In those days, Peter stood up among the believers (a group numbering about a hundred and twenty) and said, "Brothers, the

Scriptures had to be fulfilled which the Holy Spirit spoke long ago through the mouth of David concerning Judas, who served as guide for those who arrested Jesus—he was one of the number and shared in this ministry. Peter said, "For it is written in the book of Psalms, 'May his place be deserted; let there be no one to dwell in it, and may another take his place of leadership.' Therefore it is necessary to choose one of the men who have been with us the whole time the Lord Jesus went in and out among us, beginning from John's baptism to the time when Jesus was taken up from us. For one of these must become a witness with us of His resurrection."

So they propose two men: Joseph called Barsabas (also known as Justus) and Matthias. Then they prayed, "Lord, You know everyone's heart. Show us which of these two You have chosen to take over this apostolic ministry, which Judas left to go where he belongs." Then they cast lots, and the lot fell to Mathias; so he was added to the eleven apostles.

When the day of Pentecost came, they were all together in one place. Suddenly a sound like the blowing of a violent wind came from heaven and filled the whole house where they were sitting. They saw what seemed to be tongues of fire that separated and came to rest on each of them. All of them were filled with the Holy Spirit and began to speak in other tongues as the Spirit enabled them.

48. *Day 50 – Peter's Sermon* (Acts 2:14–40)

Church Interpretation: Peter's sermon focuses on two prophetic themes: (1) the promised coming of the Holy Spirit, and (2) The Resurrection of Christ from the dead. The pattern of showing Old Testament prophecy fulfilled in Christ, as was displayed by Peter here, is a major theme of Apostolic preaching, leading to repentance, baptism for the remission of sins, and the receiving of the Holy Spirit.

49. *Day 50 – The First Church* (Acts 2:37–42)

Now when the people heard this from Peter, they were cut to the heart, and said to Peter and the rest of the apostles, "Men and brethren, what shall we do?" Then Peter said to them, "Repent, and let everyone of you be baptized in the name of Jesus Christ for the remission of sins; and you shall receive the gift of the Holy Spirit. For the promise is to you and your children, and to all who are afar off, as many as the Lord our God will call." And with many other words he testified and exhorted them saying, "Be saved from this perverse generation."

Then those who gladly received the word were baptized; and that day about three thousand souls were added. And they continued steadfastly in the apostles' doctrine and fellowship, in the breaking of bread, and in prayers.

Chapter 5
HISTORICAL ADVANCEMENT OF THE DIVINE LITURGY

Establishment of the Christian Church

Forty days after the Resurrection, Christ assembled His disciples in Jerusalem before His Ascension, and commanded them to remain there until the Holy Spirit was sent from heaven to empower them to share the good news of salvation. Ten days later on *Pentecost*, the Holy Spirit to the disciples in Jerusalem and the Church was established. The first Christian community was started that day in Jerusalem, when Peter gave the first sermon, and more than three thousand people were baptized into the faith. During the period that the apostles spread the Word throughout the region, and beyond, a form of church Eucharistic service was established.

By 50 AD the Church took on the role as an international Church at a meeting of the apostles and other leaders in Jerusalem. At that meeting, which was considered the first council meeting or synod of the Church, a consensus was reached to allow Gentiles to become members of the faith.

The Development of Liturgical Structure

The institution of the sacrament of the Holy Eucharist, or Holy Communion, took place at the Last Supper. The Christian worship services were originally called the Love Feast or Holy Eucharist Service, and they were a dramatic reenactment of the Last Supper and the life of Christ. The leader or clergyman of highest rank would recite the words of Christ, "Take eat; this is my body. Drink from it all of you, for this is my blood of the new covenant, which is shed for many for the forgiveness of sins." Then they would ask the Holy Spirit to change the offered bread and wine into the body and blood of Christ so that all baptized Christians would receive Holy Communion.

The early services covered the ministry of Christ, the Last Supper, the resurrection, and the Holy Eucharist. The services began with psalms, hymns, and readings from the Old Testament. The four Gospels and the Epistles—as they are known in the modern Bible—were written before 100 AD. However, the twenty-seven books of the New Testament were not assembled and incorporated into the liturgical services until after 300 AD, the time of Constantine the Great and the start of the New Roman Empire.

Christians first worshiped in the synagogues. After Jewish leaders prohibited Christians from entering temples, worship services were held in private homes. During the persecution of the Christians by the Roman Emperors (100–300 AD), services were held in catacombs, cemeteries, basements, and other secluded areas.

The Teaching of the Twelve Apostles, written between 100 and 130 AD, documented a form for conducting the Liturgy. Although the author of this work is unknown, he confirms that the central focus was the Eucharistic as sacrifice. Writing during the same period, the Roman author Pliny confirms that Christians worshiped on a fixed day—Sunday—and sang hymns to Christ whom they worshiped "as a God". In *First Apology and Dialogue with Trypho,* Justin Martyr is more specific and indicates that the Liturgy in 150 AD had the following parts:

1. Readings from the Old Testament
2. A sermon
3. Prayers said on behalf of all people
4. The kiss of peace
5. The presentation of the bread and cup to the leader of the service (i.e., an offertory)

6. Prayers of praise and thanksgiving offered over the gifts of bread and wine
7. The administration of the elements of the sacrament by deacons to the baptized Christians
8. The collections of donations for the poor

In 350 AD, the *Sacramentary of Serapion* was written as a guide for the people to participate in the service. This guide had well defined sections and elements. The sacramentary is similar to modern books for *litourgia*—meaning public work done for the benefit of others—and divides the service of the Eucharist (now called the Divine Liturgy) into two distinct parts: the service for the catechumens and the service for the faithful. The catechumens are those that have not been baptized in the name of the Father, the Son, and the Holy Spirit. The faithful could participate in the entire Liturgy, but the catechumens could not. By this time, the New Testament had been canonized and, according to Serapion, readings were incorporated into the Liturgy. Serapion identifies the service structure as follows:

I. The Liturgy of the Catechumens:
1. The first prayer of the Trisagion (Holy God, Holy Mighty, Holy Immortal, have mercy on us)
2. Readings from the holy Gospel
3. The sermon
4. Prayers after the sermon
5. Prayers for the catechumens
   At this point, the catechumens would depart and the worship would continue with:
II The Liturgy of the Faithful:
1. The Hymn "Holy, Holy, Holy, Lord God of Hosts…"
2. The "Anamnesis" or remembrance of the events and words by which the Sacrament was founded. "Take eat, this is my body. Drink from it all of you, for this is my blood of the new covenant, which is shed for many for the forgiveness of sins."

3. The "Epiclesis," which is the calling upon God to bless and consecrate the gifts
4. The commemoration of the dead
5. The Communion
6. The concluding and dismissal prayers

Earlier documents likewise referenced these same integral parts as well as the two-part structure. Indeed, it is within this historical structure that subsequent liturgies were developed in the next century, including the liturgies we use today—those of St. John Chrysostom, St. Basil, St. James, and the pre-sanctified. It is fairly easy to recognize that today's Liturgy is no stranger to the elements of those early liturgies.

Once Christianity became a permitted religion in 313 A.D during the reign of Constantine the Great, large numbers of people openly sought out instruction and participation in the Church and public worship. The Church sought a practical solution to the influx of followers—instruction of the catechumens during the first part of the Liturgy. As a result, the Scripture readings, sermon, and a form of the creed, which we still say today, were incorporated into the first part of the Liturgy. Thereafter, those who were not baptized members were dismissed, since they could not participate in the remainder of the service—which includes the offering and receipt of the Holy Eucharist.

While we no longer dismiss those who are not of our faith during the course of the Liturgy, *the generalized structure (and constraints on the receipt of the Sacrament) remain the same up through today.*

The Proskomide (Preparation of the Bread and Wine)

While the preparation of the bread and wine took place during the celebration of the early Liturgy that is not the case today. Indeed, Justin Martyr's liturgical description of about 150–200 A. D. describes the Proskomide, also referred to as the "Liturgy of the Oblation," as taking place after the Liturgy of the Catechumens and before the Liturgy of the Faithful. It was thereafter moved to the beginning of liturgical worship. Today, because it takes place during the Orthros and in a non-public fashion, most faithful worshipers are unfamiliar with it. It is however, a distinct, necessary part of liturgical worship, and has the same historical continuity as the other parts of the Liturgy previously discussed.

The Nine Parts of Today's Liturgy: "Like Pearls on a String"

In a written history of the Eastern Orthodox Church, an English author, R.M. French, describes the structure of the Divine Liturgy with particular emphasis on the hymnography of the Church. He focuses on the unique nature of the Orthodox hymns, their construction, poetry, and their instructive and moralizing nature. He identifies that the hymns function as signals that separate distinct parts of the Divine Liturgy. He further characterizes them as being strung together, serving a specific purpose, yet able to be viewed as part of a larger structure "like pearls on a string."

The patterns, distinctions and makeup of the Liturgy, with recognizable units of identification, act as the "pearls on a string" for us. The litanies (e.g., Lord Have Mercy, Grant This to Us O Lord), which are often repeated and are similar to refrains in music, will assist us in discerning the various patterns and sections of the Divine Liturgy. The nine clearly defined segments of the Divine Liturgy of St. John Chrysostom are as follows:

1. **Litany of Peace** – Prayers to the Lord, starting with "*In peace let us pray to the Lord*," followed by "*Lord Have Mercy (Kyrieleison*" for each prayer.
2. **First Antiphon*** – "*Through the prayers of the Theotokos (Tes Presvies).*"
3. **Second Antiphon** – "*Save us O Son of God (Soson Imas),*" followed by; "*Only begotten Son (O Monogenis Yios).*"
4. **Third Antiphon (Small Entrance)** – Dismissal Hymn of the Day followed by "*Come let us worship (Thevte proskeinisomen*)," followed by the hymn of the Church and other appointed hymns.

5. **Scripture Reading**** – Begins with the **Trisagion** Prayer (Holy God, Holy Mighty, Holy Immortal), then the Epistle and Gospel are read.

6. **Great Entrance** – Begins with the prayer *"Again we bow before you, our Loving God,"* followed by the singing of the **Cherubic Hymn** (Oita Cheruveim): the **prosphoro** (bread) and wine are transferred from the Table of Preparation to the Holy Table.

7. **Great Eucharistic Prayer** – This section begins with a blessing, *"Peace be to all,"* followed by *Hymn to the Trinity* and recitation of **The Nicene Creed**; the priest then begins the Eucharistic Prayer, *"It is proper and right...,"* and then describes the angelic hosts *"singing, crying out, proclaiming the triumphal hymn;"* the choir then responds by chanting "Holy, Holy, Holy (Agios, Agios, Agios)." The Eucharistic prayer proceeds to where the priest repeats the words by which Christ established the Sacrament of Holy Communion, *"Take eat; this is my body, which is broken for you for the forgiveness of sins." "Likewise, he took the cup after supper saying: 'Drink of it, all of you; this is my blood of the New Testament, which is shed for you and for many, for the forgiveness of sins.'"* The gifts are offered and consecrated as the faithful kneel and the choir chants with moving adoration, We Praise You (Se Ymnoumen). As the priest recites the last part of the Eucharistic prayer, the choir chants praises to the Mother of God: "Truly You Are (Axion Estin)." After the Great Eucharistic Prayer comes to an end, the congregation recites the **Lord's Prayer**. The largest section of the Liturgy, which is the heart of liturgical action, comes to an end.

8. **Holy Communion** – The most valuable section of the Liturgy begins with the priest saying, *"The Holy Gifts for those who are holy."* The choir reminds us that there is only one who measures up to that obligation: "One is

Holy, One is Lord, Jesus Christ (Eis Agios)." The gifts are elevated and the priest is the first one to receive Holy Communion while the choir sings the Communion Anthem: "Praise the Lord (Aineite Ton Kyrion)." The priest makes the Call to Communion, *"With fear of God, faith and love, come forward."* The believers receive Holy Communion. After Communion the priest raises the chalice and says, *"O God, save your people and bless your inheritance."* The choir expresses the joy for the laity by chanting, "We Have Seen the Light (Eithomen to Fos)." This section ends with the Prayer of Thanksgiving, *"We thank you, Loving Master,..."*

9. **Dismissal** – The final section of the Divine Liturgy gets underway with the priest giving the instructions to the faithful, *"Let us go forth in peace."* The choir sings Lord Have Mercy three times and calls upon the priest with the words, "Holy Father give the blessing." The priest responds with the prayer, *"Lord, bless those who bless you and sanctify those who put their trust in you. Save your people..."* The choir responds joyfully and gratefully with words of praise for the priest, "Blessed Be The Name (Eie To Onoma)." The priest then calls upon all the saints to intercede for the faithful and the choir sings a prayer on behalf of the priest to protect, "He Who Blesses Us (Ton Evlogounta)." The Divine Liturgy concludes with the same words that close every other Orthodox Christian service: *"Through the prayers of our Holy Fathers, Lord Jesus Christ our God, have mercy on us and save us."*

*Antiphon – A hymn or verse from psalms or other books, sung in alternating responsive parts.

**The Apostolic Constitutions, written around 170 AD indicate that the Liturgy of the Catechumens concludes at this point, and the Liturgy of the Faithful begins.

Having identified and comprehended these nine segments, one is then prepared to consider and grasp each element's purpose and significance. Further reflection allows a deeper understanding of what the Liturgy requires of each of us—and how we can all participate.

The Divine Liturgy is organized in such a manner so as to lead the worshipers step by step through the awesome events of Holy Communion. The priest and laity come together as the CHURCH, and together, as the CHURCH they perform the Liturgy. Afterward, we have to follow through and show that the Liturgy has touched our lives. "Let us go forth in peace" is a call for us to better ourselves, to serve the world around us, and to bear witness to the Good News of Jesus Christ to all.

Chapter 6

HARMONY OF PRIESTS AND BELIEVERS IN THE DIVINE LITURGY

It is a great privilege and a blessing to be a part of the Christian Church that has direct historical connection and continuity with our Lord Jesus Christ, His appointed disciples and apostles, the early Church Fathers, and the seven ecumenical councils. The Orthodox Church has maintained the integrity of the Divine Liturgy, the Church canons and doctrines, and the holy traditions throughout the many centuries that have passed since our Lord through the Holy Spirit ordained His disciples and established the Church on the day we now celebrate as Pentecost.

Since the fourth century, there has been little change in the Divine Liturgy celebrated in the Orthodox Church of today, so that it truly expresses what the apostles and the early Church Fathers had originally established. *The Divine Liturgy is a remembrance of the life of Christ!* It is important that one join in this sacred celebration and *totally participates* in this Holy Eucharist service. Truly, the Holy Spirit empowered the apostles and early Church Fathers in formulating and establishing the Divine Liturgy so that each of us can experience communion with Christ through the Holy Eucharist.

The entire Divine Liturgy is organized so that it might lead the worshipers step by step through the awesome events of Holy Communion. Written using powerful dialogue between the priest, who offers the sacrifice, and the believers who participate, *the priest and laity come together as the CHURCH.*

For such a union to occur, the priest and worshipers must join in *harmony* at all times for the CHURCH to perform the Divine Liturgy. The priest performs the Liturgy but the emphasis is on the people's participation. Each believer must act, must participate, must pray the Liturgy. However, for the people to fully accomplish this, each passage, each prayer, each hymn, each Litany, each statement, each dialogue in the Liturgy must be communicated in a language understandable and meaningful to the participant. The priest must perform the Liturgy so that there is no disruption in the *harmony* between him and the people.

A Challenge to the Church

To truly participate in the Liturgy one must involve as many of their senses as possible, including seeing (observing and reading), hearing (embracing the unified voices), feeling (sensing that our Lord is present with us), and speaking (singing hymns, repeating prayers, etc.). Integrating all of the senses allows one to be totally absorbed in the Liturgy. For example, if one is listening and reading at the same time, and in a shared language, the thought and concentration processes are merged effectively. If there is a distraction of one of the senses, such as a baby crying, it interrupts the hearing, and thus the overall sensory process. Or if the hearing is impacted by a change of language that one does not comprehend, such as the priest changes from English to biblical Greek for long statements of faith—this causes a separation between the reading and listening processes, and interrupts the continuity of the sensory process and one's concentration. Once the priest returns to the English language, it will probably take several passages before one is able to restore complete concentration on the Liturgy once again. It is easy to imagine the degree of interruptions and distortions inevitable if there are no books available in the pews to translate the passages for which biblical Greek is used.

The clergy and hierarchy continually emphasize that members should regularly attend and participate in the Holy Eucharist services. At the same time in some communities, the use of biblical Greek is used in many parts of the services, which distracts many from total participation. St. Paul says in his letter to the Corinthians, "So likewise you, unless you utter by the tongue words easy to understand, how will it be known what is spoken?"(See 1 Cor. 14:9) "For if I pray in a foreign tongue, my spirit prays, but my understanding is unfruitful" (1 Cor. 14:14). "Yet in the church I would rather speak five words with my understanding, that I may teach others also, than ten thousand words in a foreign tongue" (1 Cor. 14:19).

There has been slow progress in using English in the church services in America for the Greek Orthodox Church. It is true that in recent years more English has been used in the Sunday Liturgies. However, in many churches a major portion of the Matins, Vespers, Pre-sanctified Liturgies, Compline Services, and the Holy Week Services are still mainly presented in biblical Greek. At this point, there are no translation books readily available in the pews (some can be individually ordered) for these services.

What is the reason that the hierarchy continues to sanction that part of the Divine Liturgy, or substantial portions of some of other services, use biblical Greek? It is understandable that the congregations in America were essentially all immigrant Greeks in the early 1900s. However, we are now well into the fourth and fifth generations, many of whom don't even understand Modern Greek. In addition, about 90 percent of marriages in the Greek Orthodox Church today are mixed marriages. Converts now constitute a significant portion of our current membership. The above arguments provide still more reasons why the language of all the church services should be essentially in English.

During the tenth century, the brothers Saint Cyril and Saint Methodius were sent to the Slavic countries by the ecumenical patriarch to convert the mostly pagan population to Christianity. They had obtained a good understanding of the Slavic dialect in their childhood. The conversion of the Slavs from pagans to Christians was accomplished by using a language that the population would understand. The fact is that Cyril and Methodius also established and organized the Slavic alphabet, which the Slavs had not had up to that point. The conversion to Orthodox Christianity of all those Slavic countries—Russia, Serbia, Bulgaria, Rumania, etc.—would not have been successful if the services, the gospels, and other church materials containing the doctrines and dogmas of the Church, had not been translated from Greek to the Slavic language. Why have we not yet converted all the church services to the English language and formed one Orthodox Church from all the ethnic Orthodox Churches here in America?

Most Greeks immigrating to America have very little, if any understanding of the biblical Greek language due to the variances of the two dialects. One may see many of those individuals reading the books of translation during the services once they learn how to read English. In recent years, Greece has discussed converting the language of the church services to Modern Greek. These changes are beginning to occur.

It took me years of reading books, attending seminars, and watching videotapes, for me to begin to acquire some understanding of our Liturgy. The language of the Divine Liturgy during my youth, and even later years, was all biblical Greek. My mother, originally from Greece, was a good example for me as I used to see her reading religious books in the Modern Greek language every night in order to learn more about her Greek Orthodox faith, and especially the Church and the liturgical services. My own efforts involved asking questions in our *catichico scholio* of the Greek School, with little success because our Greek School used only the Modern Greek language. Further perception was realized when the books of translation for the Sunday liturgies were published and placed in the pews. But a more complete understanding and a greater feeling of participation came about when a large portion of the Sunday liturgical services applied English.

I think it's time that our American church leaders focus more on Church traditions instead of Greek ethnic traditions. They should establish means where believers join *in complete harmony* with the priest at each liturgical service. This would require using to a greater degree a common language. It is the responsibility of our church leaders to take action toward that direction. *Also to the same extent having one Orthodox Church in America with a common language should also be the ultimate goal of all church leaders in America.*

Chapter 7
A GUIDE TO ORTHODOX CHRISTIANITY FAITH AND WORSHIP

About the Orthodox Christian Church

The Greek Orthodox or Eastern Orthodox Church believes that it is the One, Holy, Catholic (universal), and Apostolic Church. The word "Orthodox" signifies the right belief in the eternal truths as taught by Jesus and the apostles. The word "Greek," as in Greek Orthodox, suggests the contributions of Hellenism to Christianity during the early Church growth. It is a historical rather than an ethnic reference.

One may ask, is the Orthodox Church a true Church of Christ? The church's origins would imply yes, because it was founded by Christ and has maintained a living connection to the original early Church over the centuries. The Orthodox Church has wholly embraced the faith of the apostles as contained in both the Holy Scriptures and sacred traditions as interpreted by the Church Fathers and as lived and maintained by the Church throughout the centuries. Thus the Greek Orthodox Church—also known as the Eastern Orthodox Church—we speak with confidence when we claim uninterrupted continuity with the early Church of the apostles.

More recently theologians, clergyman, and laymen from various Christian faiths have come to the conclusion that the Orthodox Church today is the one Christian Church with an accountable historical connection to the early Church. A substantial number of priests, ministers, and church groups from other Christian denominations have converted to Orthodox Christianity these last few decades because of this historical connection. Yet the question remains: How can the Orthodox Church make the claim to be the One, Holy, Catholic, and Apostolic Church?

1. It is one in doctrine, beliefs, and dogma.
2. It is holy since Christ and the Holy Spirit ordained it on the day of Pentecost.
3. It is catholic because it is universal.
4. The Greek Orthodox Church is apostolic—meaning the bishops and clergy have uninterrupted succession with the apostles (Apostolic Succession).

The Orthodox Church is comprised of various autonomous or autocephalous national churches and patriarchates, with nearly 300 million followers worldwide. Although certain cultural or ethnic divergences among the ethnic Orthodox Churches are permitted—the doctrines, dogmas, and theology are one. The Church as a whole is infallible, not any one particular leader. The Church holds the original seven ecumenical councils as an important part of sacred tradition. Since the councils themselves originally depended on the approval of the people, today it is also the people and not the clergy alone who constitute the basis of the Orthodox Church.

If any of us Orthodox Christians carefully examine the history of Christianity, we will also come to the conclusion, like many others, that the Orthodox Church of today is a true Church of Christ (see chapters 1 & 2). However, this knowledge does not imply that Orthodox Christians have achieved perfection; as humans we have many personal shortcomings. Trying to achieve the goal of *Theosis*, or becoming Christ-like, is a life-long struggle, because as humans we are imperfect and only *Christ was perfect*. We have to continually make our best effort in gaining the greatest understanding of what Christ is trying to teach us through the faith and worship of our Orthodox Church.

Orthodox worship, especially as related to the Divine Liturgy, is nothing less than a witness to history. It recalls particular historical events not only from Jesus's life on earth, but also from the life of the Church, the saints, martyrs, and theologians. Dogma, doctrines, and creed are all part of the church's liturgical life. The Holy Liturgy belongs to all the faithful. The Nicene Creed, spoken at every Liturgy, declares the total beliefs of the Orthodox doctrine. Every hymn sung during the Liturgy is a statement of faith, a lesson in theology. It has been said that those who wish to know about Orthodoxy should not so much read books, but should attend, understand, and participate in the Divine Liturgy.

Divine Liturgy and Eucharistic Worship Celebration

Ninth century emissaries were sent by Prince Vladimir of Russia (at that time a pagan) to investigate the major religions of the world. Upon returning and reporting their investigations, they said in their report "that when they attended the Divine Liturgy at Agia Sophia in Constantinople, they did not know whether they were on earth or in heaven" How does one become a part of this sacred celebration and participate in the Divine Liturgy to the extent where one can't tell whether on earth or in heaven?

Foremost, an Orthodox Christian must come to the belief that he is part of the Church that has maintained the identity of the original Church started by Christ. The Divine Liturgy celebrated in the Orthodox Church of today has been essentially unchanged since the fourth century, in order to truly express what the apostles and early Church Fathers had originally established. Knowing this, one should do more than regularly attend the Holy Eucharistic Service. One not only has to comprehend the prayers and hymns, but also must gain a thorough understanding of the story the Liturgy is trying to teach us. *One has to genuinely participate in the Divine Liturgy!*

When you do get to the point of faithfully following and participating in the Liturgy, you begin to understand the various prayers more thoroughly. The Liturgy is a constant learning process as the priest says the beatitudes, the psalms, and other statements of faith. There is a message in each of the church's hymns. You begin to realize that each Epistle reading has a purpose and lesson to it.

Each gospel reading describes either an episode in the life of Christ or one of Christ's parables. You state the total beliefs of the Church when you recite the Nicene Creed. As you proceed through the Liturgy you venture through the various events of Christ's life—His ministry, His death, burial, resurrection, and ascension. Finally you are at the Last Supper! As the priest repeats what Christ Himself said, one truly feels the Holy Spirit descending as it did almost two thousand years ago as it changes the bread and wine into the body and blood of Christ. After receiving Holy Communion, you feel that you are in Christ and Christ is in you. You feel that you have suffered with Christ and have been resurrected with renewed spirit. It is an experience without equal

The Divine Liturgy Service

Major Divine Liturgy Celebrations

A. St. John Chrysostom – The normal Liturgy celebrated on Sundays and Holidays

B. St. Basil – Used ten times a year during Lent. Similar to St. John Chrysostom except for some of the prayers, most of which are greater in length

C. Liturgy of the Pre-sanctified – A combined Liturgy and Vesper Service, used Wednesdays during Lent; there is no consecration of the bread and wine in this Liturgy; Communion is given using elements consecrated the previous Sunday

D. St. James – Celebrated twice a year

What Is the Divine Liturgy?

1. The word *Liturgy* (from the Greek word *Litourgia*) means "a common service of a mass of people."

2. The Orthodox Divine Liturgy is a mystical action between God and man that originated with the Last Supper. There have been no substantial changes since the fourth century in the Orthodox Christian liturgical worship.

3. The Liturgy is a remembrance of the life of Christ. It is like a play or movie of the life of Jesus.
4. What Jesus said and did two thousand years ago happen again before our eyes in the Liturgy. We are there when these great events actually happened. We sense that we are moving toward God and God is moving toward us.
5. We believe that through the great sacrament of Holy Communion, or Eucharist (from the Greek word *efcharistos*—meaning "profound thanks"), the Lord comes to be born in us. We are united as members of His Church of Christ.
6. In the first part of the Liturgy, the Liturgy of the Word, we receive the Word of God. He gives us His instructions in the Epistle lesson and the gospel lesson.
7. In the second part of the Liturgy, the Liturgy of the Faith, or the Eucharist we receive the power of God through the Holy Spirit.

Abridged Version of the Divine Liturgy of St. John Chrysostom

Following is an abridged version of The Divine Liturgy of St. John Chrysosotom. The nine parts of the Liturgy are expanded in this version so that all the actual segments and parts of the Liturgy are included. The source used was compiled and translated by the Rev. Alexander Leondis, Rev. Socrates Tsamulatis, and Rev. James Moulketis.

A. Liturgy of the Word – Part 1

1. OPENING PRAYER – The priest begins the Liturgy saying: "**Blessed is the Kingdom of the Father and of the Son and of the Holy Spirit**"
(God is the eternal King. All those who live according to His will make up His Kingdom starting here on earth and which is to be completed in heaven).
2. GREAT LITANY – Prayers of peace followed by **"Lord Have Mercy (Kyrie Eleison)."**

Followed by the prayer in remembrance of our most holy, pure, blessed and glorious Lady Theotokos. Conclude with the Hymn to the Mother of God: (Tes Presvies Tin Theotokou) – **"Through the Prayers of the Theotokos Savior Save Us."**

3. SMALL LITANY – Prayer of peace followed by **"Lord Have Mercy."** Followed by the prayers for God to have mercy on us and protect us; and in remembrance of our most holy, pure, blessed and glorious Lady Theotokos. Followed by the Hymn to the Savior (**"Save us O Son of God…"**) and the hymn, **"Only Begotten Son…"**. Followed by the prayer in remembrance of our most holy, pure, blessed and glorious Lady Theotokos. Conclude with prayers glorifying Father, Son, and Holy Spirit.

4. PROCESSION OF THE SMALL ENTRANCE – The Dismissal Hymn of the Day is sung. The priest brings the gospel out to the congregation saying, **"Wisdom let us attend."** (He comes out to announce the coming of Christ to speak to us all His truths and the wisdom of God.) The faithful bow their heads and sing – **"Come let us worship and bow down before Christ our Lord. Save us, O Son of God, who did rise from the dead who sing to you. Alleluia."**
The dismissal hymn of the Church is sung, followed by other appointed hymn(s) and kontakion.

5. PRAYER OF THE THRICE HOLY HYMN – The priest says the prayer before the Thrice Holy Hymn. **"O holy God, you dwell among your saints. You are praised by the Seraphim with the thrice-holy hymn. You are glorified by the cheribum and worshiped by all the heavenly powers. You created all things from nothingness. You created man in your image and likeness and adorned him with all your gifts. You give wisdom and understanding to him who asks and do not overlook the sinner, but have provided repentance as the way to salvation. You made us**

worthy, your humble and unworthy servants, to stand at this time before the glory of your holy altar and to offer the proper worship and praise. Lord accept the thrice-holy hymn also from the mouths of us sinners and visit us in your goodness. Forgive us our sins, intentional and unintentional, sanctify our souls and bodies and grant that we may worship you in holiness all the days of our lives. This we ask through the prayers of the holy Theotokos and all the saints who have pleased you throughout the ages. For you our God, are holy and to you we offer glory to the Father, and the Son and the Holy Spirit, now and forever and to the ages of ages."** Followed by the chanting of the Thrice Holy Hymn (Trisagion) – **"Holy God, Holy Mighty, Holy Immortal have mercy on us" (three times).**

6. THE EPISTLE – A passage is read from the Letters of St. Paul or from St. James, St. Peter, St. John, St. Jude or from the Acts of the Apostles. The words of the Epistles are admonitions based on the life of Christ. The reading is followed by the chant **"Alleluia, Alleluia, Alleluia."**

7. PRAYER BEFORE THE GOSPEL – Congregational prayer: "**Master, who loves us, shine your eternal light in our hearts that we may better know you. Help us to fully understand your gospel message. Instill in us respect for your Holy Commandments, that by overcoming our worldly desires we might live a spiritual life of thoughts and deeds, which pleases you. We ask this of you, O Christ our God, for you are the light of our souls and bodies and to you we offer glory with your eternal Father and your all-holy, good and life-giving Spirit, now and forever and to the ages of ages, AMEN."**

8. THE HOLY GOSPEL – The priest announces, **"Wisdom. Let us stand to hear the holy gospel. Peace be with you."**

Each gospel lesson is taken from one of the four evangelists – Matthew, Mark, Luke, and John. It describes either an episode in the life of Christ or one of Christ's parables. The gospel reading is preceded and followed by the hymn **"Glory to You O God, glory to You."**

B. Liturgy of the Faithful or Holy Eucharist – Part 2

1. THE GREAT ENTRANCE – The priest prepares for the Procession of the Great Entrance by saying the prayer, **"Again we bow before you, our loving God, and ask that you hear our prayer. Cleanse our souls and bodies from sin. Allow us to stand innocently before your holy altar. Grant us spiritual growth, faith and understanding. Allow us to worship you at all times with love and respect. Make us worthy to receive your holy mysteries and to inherit your heavenly kingdom."**

   "Grant that always being protected by your power, we may glorify you the Father, the Son, and the Holy Spirit, now and forever and to the ages of ages."

2. THE CHERUBIC HYMN (Oita Cherouvim) – The people chant **"Amen. We who mystically represent the cherubim, sing the thrice holy hymn to the Life-giving Trinity. Let us put away all worldly cares, so that we may receive the King of all."**

3. PROCESSION OF THE GREAT ENTRANCE – The priest carries out the gifts (bread and wine) and places them on the Holy Table. It reminds us of Jesus on His way to the cross. We are in Calgary! We are also the thief who repented as the priest says the prayer, **"Remember O Lord each of us in your Kingdom."** (During the Great Entrance Christ mystically enters our lives to offer

the eternal sacrifice for our salvation and lead us into the presence of God.)

4. OFFERATORY PRAYER – The priest says the prayer, **"Lord God Almighty, you alone are holy and accept the offering of praise from those who call upon you with all their heart. Accept also the prayer of us sinners at your altar. Enable us to offer to you gifts and spiritual sacrifices for our sins and for the errors of the people. Make us worthy to find grace before you, that our offering may please you and that the good Spirit of your grace may come upon us, upon these gifts and all your people."**

5. EXCHANGE OF PEACE – The priest blesses the faithful saying, **"Peace be with you."**

6. MOVEMENT OF LOVE – The priest then says to the people: **"Let us love one another that we may in one mind confess."** The choir responds by chanting the Hymn to the Trinity: **"The Father and Son and Holy Spirit one in essence, and inseparable."**

7. THE NICENE CREED – The priest declares, **"Christ is among us."** Response by congregation: **"He is and shall always be."** The congregation then recites the **Nicene Creed.**

8. THE OFFERING OF THE HOLY GIFTS – The priest says **"Let us stand reverently and respectfully; let us be attentive, that we may offer the Holy Gifts in peace."** (At this point we raise our minds and lift up our hearts to the Heavenly Father and thank Him for his infinite blessing.) The priest continues with brief prayers to the Lord with a response from the Choir after each prayer. The priest then begins the prayer praising the Lord: **"It is proper and right to praise you, to bless you, to offer you glory…"** Gratefully the choir and the people chant along with the angels and archangels the triumphant hymn, Agios, Agios, Agios, **"Holy, Holy, Holy, Lord of Angelic Hosts, heaven and earth are**

full of glory. O blessed is He who comes in the name of the Lord."

9. THE EUCHARISTIC PRAYER – We are at the Last Supper! The priest repeats what Christ said two thousand years ago: **"Take eat. This is my Body which is broken for you for the forgiveness of sins. Drink of it, all of you. This is my Blood which is shed for you for the forgiveness of sins."** The priest then calls to mind Christ's death, burial, Resurrection, Ascension, and Second Coming. He offers the Holy Gifts in peace. The faithful kneel.

10. THE CONSECRATION: EPICLESIS OR KNEELING PRAYER – The priests asks for the calling down of the Holy Spirit to consecrate the Holy Gifts. **"And make this bread the precious body of thy Christ. Amen. And that which is in this cup, the precious blood of thy Christ. Amen. Changing them by thy Holy Spirit. Amen. Amen, Amen."** During this consecration of the Holy Gifts the congregation with deep spiritual connection, while kneeling, chants the hymn along with the choir, **"We praise Thee, we bless Thee, we give thanks to thee, O Lord"** (Se Eimnoumen).

11. GREAT COMMERATION – We especially commemorate the mother of God. The hymn "Truly You Are" (Axion Estin) is chanted. We commemorate the saints, Church leaders, and all those who have fallen asleep.

12. SUPPLICATION FOR THE CONSECRATED GIFTS – Congregational prayer: **"Loving Master, we commit our life and entrust our hope to you and pray: make us worthy to receive your heavenly and awesome mysteries on this holy and spiritual altar with a clear conscience and grant us forgiveness of the Holy Spirit, the inheritance of the Kingdom in heaven, confidence to approach you, and keep us from judgment and condemnation."**

13. THE LORD'S PRAYER – The congregation recites the Lord's Prayer.

14. ELEVATION OF THE GIFTS – The priest presents the Holy Gifts. **"Let us be attentive. The Holy Gifts for those who are holy."** The hymn "One Is Holy" (Eis Agios) is chanted; **"One is holy, One is Lord, Jesus Christ our Lord; to the glory of God the Father. Amen."**

15. THE COMMUNION HYMN – Ainoite – **"Praise the Lord from the heavens, praise Him in the highest. Alleluia."**

16. PRAYERS BEFORE HOLY COMMUNION – Each communicant silently prays – **"I believe, Lord, and confess that you are truly the Christ, the Son of the Living God, who came to this world to save sinners of whom I am the first. I also believe that this is your sacred body and precious blood. I pray, therefore have mercy on me, forgive my sins, voluntary and involuntary, in word and deed, both known and unknown, and make me worthy to receive your sacred mysteries, for the forgiveness of sins and life everlasting. Amen."** (There are additional prayers to be repeated by each communicant in preparing for communion).

17. PROCESSION FOR HOLY COMMUNION –THE HOLY EUCHARIST – The priest receives Holy Communion. He then calls upon the communicants: **"With the fear of God, faith and love, come forward."** The movement of the priest from the altar to the people with the holy cup shows Christ is coming to each of us. As we receive Holy Communion the whole Christ body and blood enters our hearts and gives us new life. Following Holy Communion we sing the hymn "We Have Seen the True Light" (Eithomen to Fos): **"We have seen the true light, we have received the Heavenly**

Spirit, we have found the true faith, worshiping the undivided Trinity, who has saved us."

18. PRAYER OF THANKSGIVING – Congregational prayer. **"We thank you, loving master, benefactor of our souls, that you on this day have made us worthy to receive your heavenly and immortal mysteries. Direct us in the right way, strengthen our respect towards you, guard our lives, make our footsteps safe through the prayers of the glorious Theotokos and Ever-Virgin Mary and all the saints."**

19. DISMISSAL PRAYER – The priest repeats the prayer: **"Lord bless those who bless you and sanctify those who trust in you. Save your people and bless your inheritance. Protect the entire body of your Church. Sanctify those who love the beauty of your house. Glorify them in return by your divine power and do not abandon us who hope in you. Grant peace to your world, to the armed forces and to all your people. For every good and perfect gift comes from above, from you the Father of Lights whom we glorify, thank and worship, the Father, the Son and the Holy Spirit, now and forever, and to the ages of ages."** This prayer by the priest is followed by the chanting of the hymn "Blessed Be the Name": **"Blessed be the name of the Lord, our God from this time forth, forever and forever. The name of the Lord be forever blessed from this time forth forever and ever."**

20. CONCLUSION – Thanksgiving and final blessings by the priest. Prayer of the people for the priest by chanting the hymn, "He Who Blesses Us" (Ton Evlohounta): **"He who blesses us and sanctifies us Lord protect him for many years to come."**

Closing prayer by the priest: **"Through the prayers of our holy fathers, Lord Jesus Christ our God, have mercy on us and save us."**

21. DISTRIBUTION OF ANTIRODON TO THE FAITHFUL

NOTES:

1. Psalms and Beatitudes with spiritual hymns or Troparia are to be included as part of The Liturgy of the Word, Part 1.

2. There are additional repetitions of litanies not shown above throughout the Divine Liturgy, either in long or short form. The litanies reoccur several times to pray for peace, various needs of the Church and the people, our spiritual leaders, the departed, the sick, and so on. The response is again Kyrie Eleison, "Lord have mercy," except for one litany where the response is Paraschou Kyrie, "Grant this to us O Lord."

3. Six times during the Liturgy we have the opportunity to completely and willingly commit ourselves to Christ: "Let us commit ourselves and one another and our whole life to Christ, our God."

Chapter 8

UNITED TO CHRIST THROUGH THE TRUTH OF THE GOSPEL, THE CHURCH, AND THE SACRAMENTS

One of the tragic digressions of so-called modern religion is the presence of "churchless Christianity." The assertion is that it is Christ who saves us, not the Church, so "all you need is to believe in Jesus." It is this same belief that dismisses the significance of the Holy Sacraments as established by our Lord Jesus Christ.

Few who claim to be Orthodox Christians would argue against the statement that it is Christ who saves. For He is the eternal Son of God who assumed human flesh, and has done so "for us and for our salvation." Paul writes in 1Timothy 2:5, "For there is one God and one Mediator between God and men, the Man Christ Jesus."

But because this Mediator established the Church, which is His body, we who are joined to Him are joined to His Church as well. To say we love Christ, who is Head of the Church, and at the same time reject His body is to deny New Testament teaching.

Similarly, a good Christian has to uphold the sacraments, which Christ instituted as defined in the New Testament (see John 1:16:17). If one accepts that Jesus Christ is truly the Son of God, who teaches us using the New Testament and His apostles and disciples that abiding by the sacraments establishes communion with God, then how can anyone question the sacraments' importance in achieving eternal salvation?

The Church

As Explained in the Gospel and Acts: The first use of the word "church" in the New Testament comes in the Gospel of Matthew, when our Lord gives his approval of Peter's confession of faith and promises in chapter 16, verse 18; "Upon this rock (faith) I will build my church." To us this verse means that Jesus builds and we commit to cooperate with Him.

The Book of Acts discloses more of what Jesus meant in Matthew 16. When Peter's sermon on the day of Pentecost concludes, those present ask for guidance toward salvation: "What shall we do?" (see Acts 2:37.) Following Peter's word, they are baptized and join with the other believers—three thousand in total (Acts 2:38, 41). Thus, the Church was established as instructed by our Lord Jesus Christ.

Having been joined to Christ and His Church, these baptized believers begin living as the *body of Christ*. We find them looking after each other, using their personal resources to care for each other, and continuing in prayer and in the Eucharist (Acts 2:42–47). From this point on "the Lord added to His church daily those who were being saved" (Acts 2:47); and throughout Acts, the Church is being built as the gospel of Christ spreads. The early Church was a community of prayer and worship centered on the mysteries of baptism and the Lord's Supper—the Holy Eucharist (Acts 2:38,42; 8:36–38; Rom. 6:3–11; 1 Cor. 10:16,17; 11:23–29).

As Explained in the Epistles: Paul's instructions in his letters to the churches throughout the eastern Mediterranean clearly show what it means to be members of Christ—to be the Church and to be *in* the Church. Nowhere in the New Testament are Paul's teaching on the Church more fully disclosed than in Ephesians 4. In this passage, he instructs us that:

(1) The Church is *one*, "endeavoring to keep the unity of the Spirit in the bond of peace" (Eph. 4:3). There is one Church, one God, one doctrine, and one baptism.

(2) The Church consists of people, men and women, who are energized by the Holy Spirit. For "to each of us grace was given according to the measure of Christ's gift" (Eph. 4:7).

We are not all given the same gifts, but together we are equipped to do God's will.

(3) The head of the Church is *Christ*, "from whom the whole body is joined and knit together" (Eph. 4:14,16).

(4) The Church is "the new man" (Eph. 4:24), the new creation, made to be righteous and holy. We are no longer alienated from God (Eph. 4:18), but we are being renewed together (Eph. 4:23), "members of one another" (Eph. 4:25).

The Church, then, is that place established by Christ where we each may become what we are created to be, maturing and being perfected, while the Church body receives what it needs from each of us; so that it too, is perfected. The Church as the *body of Christ* carries us beyond our petty and worldly concerns, stretching our vision to the eternal and the heavenly as we ascend together to worship the Father, Son, and Holy Spirit. The Holy Sacraments, as established by Christ, are the heart of the teachings of the Church, by which its members can accept the complete mystical life of the Church and, as our Savior Jesus affirmed, achieve salvation.

The Holy Sacraments

A sacrament, or mystery, is a way in which God imparts grace to His people to bring us into closer communion with Him. Accepting these sacraments involves holy actions of the Church by which spiritual life is imparted to those receiving them. Many Christians frequently speak of seven sacraments, but God's gift of grace is not limited only to those seven—the entire life of the Church is mystical and sacramental. Christ Himself, as defined in the New Testament, instituted the seven holy sacraments as *a means for us to embrace the entire mystical life of the Church.* The Orthodox Church strongly believes in these seven mysteries, which are: baptism; chrismation (anointing); the Holy Eucharist (communion); confession; ordination; marriage; and holy unction or healing. Through the sacraments, or mysteries, God, in an act of grace, bestows *divine life* on all who live in faith and obedience, a foretaste of the fulfillment of salvation in the age to come.

The seven sacraments are discussed below with verses from the Bible that substantiate acceptance of the belief and participation in these mystical events.

Baptism: The sacrament whereby one is born again, buried with Christ, resurrected with Him, and united to Him. In baptism, one becomes a Christian and is joined by the Church. In Christ's baptism, water was set apart unto God as the means by which the Holy Spirit would bring to us new life and entrance into the heavenly Kingdom. We are raised to new life for a purpose—union and communion with God. In this deeper sense, baptism is the beginning of eternal life.

(Matt.3: 13, 16, 17) "Then Jesus came from Galilee to John at the Jordan to be baptized by him. When He had been baptized, Jesus came up immediately from the water; and behold, the heavens were opened to Him, and He saw the Spirit of God descending like a dove and alighting upon Him. And suddenly a voice came from heaven, saying, **'This is My beloved Son, in whom I am well pleased.'"**

(Matth.28: 18–20) "Jesus from the mountain came and spoke to His eleven disciples; **'All authority has been given to Me in heaven and on earth. Go therefore and make disciples of all nations, baptizing them in the name of the Father and of the Son and of the Holy Spirit; teaching them to observe all things that I have commanded you.'"**

(Rom. 6:4) "Therefore we were buried with Him through baptism into death, that just as Christ was raised from the dead by the glory of the Father, even so we also should walk in newness of life."

(Gal. 3:26, 27) "For you are all sons of God through faith in Christ Jesus. For as many of you as were baptized into Christ have put on Christ."

Chrismation: This is the sacrament completing baptism, whereby one receives the gift of the Holy Spirit through anointing with the chrism specially prepared oil, that must be consecrated by a ranking member of the hierarchy. On several occasions in Acts, a baptized

Christian was anointed and received the gift of the Holy Spirit through the laying on of hands from an apostle.

(Acts 8:15–17) "When Peter and John had come down, they prayed for them that they might receive the Holy Spirit. For as yet, the Holy Spirit had fallen upon none of them. They had only been baptized in the name of the Lord Jesus. Then they laid hands upon them and they received the Holy Spirit."

(1 John 2:27) "But the anointing which you have received from Him abides in you, and you do not need that anyone teach you; but as the same anointing teaches you concerning all things, and is true, and is not a lie, and just as it has taught you, you will abide in him."

The Holy Eucharist (Communion): Communion is a common union of the most intimate kind, enjoyed by Christians uniting with God and with each other in the Church. This communal activity is especially realized in the mystery of the Holy Eucharist. Taken from a Greek word meaning "thanksgiving," *Eucharist* designates Holy Communion, the central act of Christian worship. At the Last Supper, Christ gave thanks, and embodied in the communion service is our own thanksgiving.

(1 Cor. 11:23–25) "For I received from the Lord that which I also delivered to you: that the Lord Jesus on the same night in which He was betrayed took the bread; and when He had given thanks (GR. *eucharistesas*), He broke it and said, **'Take, eat; this is My body which is broken for you; do this in remembrance of Me.'** In the same manner, He also took the cup after supper, saying, **'This cup is the new covenant in My blood. This do, as often as you drink it, in remembrance of Me.'"** With these words quoting the same words of Christ St. Paul instructs the Corinthians concerning the Eucharist, the giving of thanks.

(Luke 22:19, 20) "And Jesus took bread, gave thanks and broke it, and gave it to His disciples saying, **'This is My body which is given for you; do this in remembrance of Me.'** Likewise He also took the cup after supper, gave thanks, saying, **'This cup is the new covenant in My blood, which is shed for you.'"**

John 6:51, 53–56) And Jesus said to the people **"I am the living bread which came down from heaven. If anyone eats of this bread, he will live forever; and the bread that I shall give is My flesh, which I shall give for the life of the world."** Then Jesus said to them, **"Most assuredly, I say to you, unless you eat the flesh of the Son of Man and drink His blood, you have no life in you. Whoever eats My flesh and drinks My blood has eternal life, and I will raise him up at the last day. For My flesh is food indeed, and My blood is drink indeed. He who eats My flesh and drinks My blood abides in Me and I in him."**

Confession: This holy sacrament is the avowal or verbal witness of faith in Christ, leading to salvation; "That if you confess with your mouth the Lord Jesus and believe in your heart that God has raised Him from the dead, you will be saved." (Rom. 10:9). It is the sacrament that provides for the forgiveness of sins, whereby the repentant sinner confesses his sins to Christ in the presence of a priest, who pronounces God's absolution of those sins. The faithful are to bring their sins to God in repentance and receive cleansing and forgiveness. Thus we come before the holy icon of Christ, to whom we confess, and are guided by the priest, our spiritual father, in a cleansing inventory of our lives. When we tell God all, naming our sins and failures, we hear those glorious words of freedom announcing Christ's promise of forgiveness of all our sins. We resolve to "go and sin no more" in John 8:11.

King David learned a lesson regarding his sin. For about a year, he had hidden his sins of adultery with Bathsheba and the murder of her husband (2 Sam. 11:1–12:3). When confronted by Nathan the prophet, David repented from his heart and confessed his sin in a psalm, which is used for general confession to this day (Psalm 51). At the point of confession, the joy of salvation was restored to him.

(1John 1:8, 9) "If we say that we have no sin, we deceive ourselves, and the truth is not in us. If we confess our sins, He is faithful and just to forgive our sins and to cleanse us from unrighteousness."

(Romans 10:9) "If you confess with your mouth the Lord Jesus and believe in your heart that God has raised Him from the dead, you will be saved."

(John 20:22, 23) "Jesus breathed on His disciples and said to them, **'Receive the Holy Spirit. If you forgive the sins of any, they are forgiven them; if you retain the sins of any they are retained.'"**

Ordination: This is the sacramental act of setting a man apart for the ministry of the Church by the bishop's laying on of hands. The original meaning of ordination includes both election as a presbyter and imposing of hands. In His ministry, Christ ordained or "set in place," the original twelve (Mark 3:14) assuring them, **"You did not choose Me, but I chose you and appointed you that you should go and bear fruit, and that your fruit should remain"** (John 15:16). Both the New Testament and the Church Fathers recognize the twelve as the first bishops or overseers in the Church. When Judas had fallen away and the remaining disciples were considering his successor, Peter said, "Let another take his office." And they cast their lots, and the lot fell on Matthias, and the laying of hands was imposed on him. And thus he was numbered with the eleven apostles in Acts 1:20, 26. The apostles these first bishops in turn ordained other presbyters and deacons. Ordination is seen as an eternal appointment, "for the gifts and the calling of God are irrevocable" (Rom. 11:29). Through the sacrament of ordination in His Church, Christ entrusts to the shepherd the very salvation of His people's souls.

(Acts 6:3–6) "Then the twelve said; 'Therefore, brethren, seek out from among you seven good men of good reputation, full of the Holy Spirit and wisdom, whom we may appoint over this business; so that we will give ourselves continually to prayer and to the ministry of the word.' And the multitude chose the seven, whom they set before the apostles; and when they had prayed, they laid hands on them."

(1 Tim. 4:14) "Timothy, do not neglect the gift that is in you, which was given to you by prophecy with the laying on of the hands of the eldership."

Marriage: The Bible and human history begin and end with weddings. Adam and Eve come together in marital union in paradise, before the Fall, revealing marriage as a part of God's eternal purpose for humanity in the midst of creation (Gen.2: 22–25). History closes with the marriage of the Bride to the Lamb (Rev. 19:7–9), earthly marriage being fulfilled in the heavenly, showing the eternal nature of the sacrament.

Between these historical events are the accounts of numerous other unions of man and wife. In the centuries-old Christian wedding ceremony used today in the Orthodox Church, several historical biblical marriages are remembered: Abraham and Sarah (Gen. 11:29–23:20); Isaac and Rebecca (Gen. 24); Joachim and Anna, parents of the Virgin Mary; and Zacharias and Elizabeth (Luke 1:5–58).

The marriage most prominently featured in the Orthodox wedding ceremony, however, is the one at Cana of Galilee, described in the Gospel passage read at every Christian Orthodox wedding (John 2:1–11). In attending this wedding and performing His first miracle there by changing water into wine, Jesus Christ, the Son of God, forever sanctifies marriage. As with all Christian sacraments, marriage is sacramental because God blesses it.

In modern society, as well as in Christendom, a recurring debate persists. The dispute deals with tension between equality of the partners in marriage and order in marriage. Often differing views turn into a polarity between men and women, and sometimes even breeds hostility. .

As to equality, the passage in Galatians 3:27, 28, defines the equality of the husband and wife as partners in marriage, and their citizenship in the Kingdom of God: "For many of you as were baptized in Christ have put on Christ. There is neither Jew nor Greek, there is neither slave nor free, there is neither male nor female; for you are all one in Christ Jesus." The words of St. Paul are clear on marital equality: "The wife does not have authority over her own body, but the husband does. And likewise also the husband does not have authority over his own body, but the wife does" (1 Cor. 7:4). Husband and wife belong to each other as martyrs, they belong to God as royalty, and they are called to treat each other accordingly.

But within marital equality there is also order. The Epistle passage read at the Orthodox Sacrament of Marriage is Ephesians 5:20–33. The exhortation to husbands and wives begins with a call "to submit to each other" (Eph 5:21). The husband is to serve God as head of his wife, just as Christ is the head of the Church (Eph. 5:23) and the wife is subject to her husband as the Church is subject to Christ (Eph. 5:24). Nothing here suggests that the wife is oppressed in marriage anymore than one would call the Church oppressed in relationship to Christ. The gospel exhorts the husband to "love his wife, to nourish and cherish her, as Christ Himself does the church" (Eph. 5:28, 29).

Thus marriage is a sacrament holy, blessed, and everlasting in the sight of God and His Church. Within the bonds of marriage, husband and wife experience a union with one another in love, and hopefully the fruit of children, and one day the joy of grandchildren. And within the bond of marriage there is both a fullness of equality between husband and wife, and clarity of order with the husband as the icon of Christ and the wife as the icon of the Church.

Holy Unction (Healing): This sacrament is the anointing of the sick with blessed oil, for the healing of body and soul. The gift of healing is bestowed by the Holy Spirit through the anointing, together with the prayers of the Unction service held on Holy Wednesday in the Orthodox Church.

"Jesus called His twelve disciples together and gave them power and authority over all demons and to cure disease. He sent them to preach the kingdom of God and to heal the sick. So they departed and went through the towns, preaching the gospel and healing everywhere" (Luke 9:1, 2, 6). The ministry of Christ was one of numerous occurrences of healings of "all kinds of sickness and all kinds of disease" (Matt. 4:23). Like their Master before them, the early apostles participated in God's work of healing as well, attributing their miracles to the risen and ascended Christ. "Jesus the Christ heals you," Peter told a newly restored man, who had been bedridden for eight years in Acts 9:34. St. Paul identified healing as a gift of the Holy Spirit (1 Cor. 12:9). Thus the New Testament foundation was established for the healing ministry to be a part of the sacramental life of the Church. "Is anyone among you sick? Let him call for the elders of the Church, and let them pray over him, anointing him with oil in the name of the Lord. And the prayer of faith will save the sick, and the Lord will raise him up. And if he has committed sin, he will be forgiven" (James 5:14, 15).

To this day, the Orthodox Church practices prayer for the sick following the New Testament instructions of St. James. The Church has a special service of healing, which may be performed at any time. The presbyter prays for the ill person, anointing him with oil and saying: **"O Lord Almighty, Healer of our souls and bodies, who puts down and raises up, who chastises and heals also, visit now in Your mercy our (name of brother, sister) _____, who is ill. Stretch forth Your arm that is full of healing and health, and raise (him, her) up from this bed, and cure this illness. Put away the spirit of disease and every malady and pain and fever. And if (he, she) has committed sins and transgressions, grant remission and forgiveness, because You love mankind."**

As Christians we pray, neither commanding God to heal nor doubting His ability to heal, pleading for His promised mercy upon all who are ill.

Belief in the Church and Sacraments through the Bible: The gospel supports the truth and accuracy about the Church and sacraments as practiced by the Orthodox Church. To be a true Christian one has to believe completely, without doubt, in the Bible. One, however, cannot preach to a congregation while waving the Bible in one hand, at the same time preach a "churchless Christianity," and exclude defining and executing the beliefs of the Holy Sacraments, which Christ Himself instituted. Christ is the Head of the Church, which is His body. Thus, if we say that we are a part of His body, then we must also accept as true that we are also joined to His Church, which insists on the seven Holy Sacraments; as described and instituted by our Lord and Savior Jesus Christ. We make the sign of the cross that our Lord suffered on when we repeat what Christ Himself told us **"In the name of the Father, Son, and Holy Spirit."**

Through the Church, Christians are united to Christ and to each other. In this community, the believer receives the grace of God through the sacraments and hears the truth of the gospel.

Chapter 9

IS JUSTIFICATION REALIZED BY FAITH ALONE?

Justification, according to Christian definition, means "being or becoming righteous." For most of Church history, justification through God's grace—*or salvation*—was seen as comprehending all of life. Christians were baptized; Christians believed in Christ; and Christians were nurtured in their salvation through the Church. Key doctrines of the faith centered around: (1) the Holy Trinity—the Father, Son, and Holy Spirit; (2) the incarnation of the Son of God—His becoming flesh, that is, human; and (3) the atonement—reconciliation of God and man through Christ and His resurrection.

This seemed to change in Western Europe during the sixteenth century, when the Reformers claimed that salvation depended on human works of merit, not upon the grace and mercy of God. On the other extreme, some religious movements experienced a redefining of justification by claiming it's not through God's grace, as defined in Paul's letter to the Romans, but achieved by faith alone.

The doctrine of justification became a storm center of the Protestant Reformation. Luther called it the doctrine upon which the Church stands or falls; Calvin declared that it was the hinge upon which all other Christian doctrines turn. The key difference between justification in classical Protestant theology and Orthodox/Catholic theology is that Protestants claim that justification is by faith alone, whereas Orthodox and Catholics claim that justification *is through grace, first channeled through the sacraments, then maintained through faith and works.*

The fundamental difference between these two theologies lies within the definition of the verb "to justify" as used in the Bible. Protestants claim that it is a forensic, or legal, *declaration* of one's righteousness. Orthodox/Catholics believe that it is in actuality *being or becoming* righteous.

Historically Luther believed that man could be saved by faith alone, which differed from being justified by faith alone. There is quite a difference between the two. Justification—being or becoming righteous—is a critical requirement in being saved, but it is not the only requirement. This, along with many other major issues, soon caused a schism between the various religious groups. (Note: See the Protestant Reformation, Chapter 3).

The Reformation debate over faith and works in the west was late breaking news for the Orthodox east, which questioned: *Why this unexpected schism of faith and works?* It had been settled by the apostles and substantiated by the original seven ecumenical councils that salvation was granted by the mercy of God to righteous men and women. Those baptized into Christ were called to believe and accept Christ, and *abide by doing good works.* A discussion of *faith versus works* was unprecedented in Orthodox thought. So what were some of the key points to the debate?

Explanation of Justification in the Bible

The Orthodox perception of justification and salvation differs from Protestant beliefs, which stem from the Reformation, in several ways:

(1) *Justification and the New Covenant:* As Orthodox Christians, when we approach the doctrine of salvation, the discussion focuses on the New Covenant. Justification (being or becoming righteous) by faith in God necessitates being brought into a covenant relationship with Him. Whereas Israel was under the Old Covenant, wherein salvation came through faith as revealed in the law, the Church is under the New Covenant, where salvation comes through faith in Christ, who fulfills the law. Thus we receive the gift of the Holy Spirit who dwells in us, leading us to the realization of God the Father. Whereas Protestant Christians focus on

justification as a lawful and instant exoneration before God, Orthodox believers see justification by faith as a covenant relationship with Him, centered in union with Christ. (See Romans 6:1–6.) We accept this as a lifelong path.

(2) *Justification and God's Mercy:* Orthodoxy emphasizes that it is first God's mercy—not our faith—that saves us. "Therefore, having been justified by faith, we have peace with God through our Lord Jesus Christ, through whom also we have access by faith into this grace in which we stand, and rejoice in hope of the glory of God" (Rom. 5:1, 2). It is God who initiates the New Covenant with us.

(3) *Justification by Faith Is Dynamic, Not Static:* For Orthodox Christians, faith is living, dynamic, continuous—never static or merely point-in-time. Faith is not something a Christian exercises only at one critical moment, expecting it to cover the rest of his life. True faith is not just a decision. True Christians make it a *way of life!*

Because of these differences in Protestant versus Orthodox understanding of justification, the modern evangelical Protestant question "Are you saved?" gives pause to Orthodox believers. As the subject of salvation is addressed in Scripture, the Orthodox Christian comprehends three aspects of salvation: *(a) I have been saved, being joined to Christ in baptism; (b) I am being saved, growing in Christ through the sacramental life of the Church; and (c) I will be saved by the mercy of God at the Last Judgment.*

A final complexity for an Orthodox Christian is the belief of *justification by faith alone.* Justification by faith, though not a major New Testament doctrine for Orthodox as it is for Protestants, poses no problem. But justification by faith *alone* brings up an objection. It contradicts Scripture, which says: "You see then that a man is also justified by works, and not by faith only" (James 2:24). We are "justified by faith apart from the deeds of the law" (Rom. 3:28). Nowhere does the Bible say we are justified by faith *alone.* On the contrary, "Faith by itself, if it does not have works, is dead" (James 2:17). Good intentions alone or faith without works will not save.

Simply to hear and not do is religion without reality. "For not the hearers of the law are just in the sight of God, but the doers of the law will be justified" (Rom. 2:13).

A more exact definition of Orthodox thinking is: *Justification is by faith received through the grace of God, followed by growing in Christ through the sacramental life of the Church and doing good works and deeds of righteousness.* This definition offers a more clear and complete explanation of the concept of justification. When we add, *"Salvation will be achieved through God's grace at the final judgment,"* we further complete the foundation. This definition offers more meaning to a Christian than simply saying, "Justification by faith alone," or being "saved by faith alone."

What exactly is meant by *faith alone*? Take the example of a cardiologist telling one of his patients who had a heart attack that the condition will necessitate heart surgery. Upon completing a successful surgery, would it be correct for the doctor to tell his patient to take required medication, neglecting to make the patient aware of other measures, such as following a strict diet, doing exercises regularly, taking periodic examinations, and following other rules that would benefit his overall healing?

As Christians we are no longer under the demands of the Old Testament law (Rom. 3:20), for Christ has fulfilled the law (Gal. 2:21; 3:5, 24). Only by God's mercy are we brought into a New Covenant relationship with Him. We who believe are granted entrance into His Kingdom by His grace. Through His mercy we are justified by faith and *empowered by God for good works or deeds of righteousness*, which bring glory to Him. Good intentions alone, or faith without works, is no guarantee it will save.

Further Explanation of Justification as Described in the Epistles of St. Paul to the Romans

If one is to truly understand the biblical doctrine of justification, Paul's epistle to the Romans is the place to go. Romans, more than any other book, proclaims the doctrinal truths of the gospel and is the most profound expression of our hope in Christ. In the first five chapters of this masterpiece, Paul lays out the need, nature, and instrument of justification. This will give us a clue as to how the Bible defines this intricate doctrine.

Paul first declares that no one can be justified on his own. He puts this in the context of the sinfulness of mankind. Romans 1:18–32 deals with the sinfulness of the Gentiles, whereas Romans 2:1–3:10 expounds upon the sinfulness of the Jews. Finally, in a grand sweeping statement, Paul declares the sinfulness of all humanity before God (Romans 3:11–3:20).

The issues that Paul discussed in each of his epistles varied depending on whom he was addressing. In Romans, Paul deals extensively with the relation of the Old Covenant to belief in Christ, and how Gentiles can be full members of the New Covenant by grace through faith. He discussed the roles of justification by faith and good works separately. But he did not mean by this that each did not have a role in being saved at the final judgment.

Sub-themes in Romans include:
(1) The natural mortality and actual sinfulness of all (1:18–3:20).
(2) Salvation through Christ apart from Mosaic Law (3:21–4:25); we live by faith in response to grace rather than by the *dead works of the law* (the Old Covenant).
(3) New life in Christ; freedom from sin, death, and the law through our sacramental identity with Christ, established in holy baptism (chapters 5–7).
(4) New life in the Holy Spirit and the power to be God-like (chapter 8).
(5) God's plan for Jews and Gentiles, and their reconciliation in Christ (chapters 9–11).
(6) Christian life in the Church and in the world (chapters 12–16).

The Epistle of Romans is Paul's most significant letter and has several qualities that set it apart from the rest of Paul's epistles. It also summarizes the entire gospel message. While most of Paul's epistles correct doctrinal or moral problems, this epistle proclaims the faith more completely and systematically, addressing few specific topics. This is probably because Paul was hoping to obtain Rome's support for his planned initial missions there and to Spain. This is the only letter Paul wrote to a church he had not yet visited.

How Do We, as Christians, Achieve Faith, Justification, and Salvation?

First, one has to start by making a commitment to have faith, and *to be faithful*. But the prevailing question remains: How do we achieve salvation by receiving the grace of God and be saved at the last judgment? Do we accomplish this by committing to faith alone and obtaining justification (being or becoming righteous)? Or is it necessary to commit to faith and ensure that we receive justification by living the life of Christ through the sacramental life of the Church, combined with doing good works and righteous deeds as we continue to make sure our commitment to faith is at the level it should be throughout our lives?

We are all human and not perfect (only Christ is perfect), so through our weaknesses we at times may not live up to God's and our own expectations. If we do fall short from time to time, we have a much better chance of being restored to the level of expected justification by: reading the Bible daily (determining whether we are carrying out Christ's instructions); praying regularly (asking for forgiveness and sanctification); and achieving God's and our expectations through the sacramental life of the Church (the Body of Christ) as our Lord commanded us.

Being saved is a step-by-step process—it is a way of life! As previously stated, the steps are: (1) *I have been saved*, being joined to Christ in baptism; (2) *I am being saved*, growing closer to Christ through the sacramental life of the church; and (3) *I will be saved* by the mercy of God at the Last Judgment. How do we come to a complete understanding of this step-by-step process so we can envision and realize that we are actually in the mode of living to achieve complete salvation?

I recall when I was in school being trained to evaluate and come to a reasonable understanding of how a series of chemical equations represent a final product. This was all part of knowing the steps in a complex chemical process. As students, we first had to go through each equation, or each step, separately to begin to attain the foundational knowledge. However, we could not come to a complete understanding of the total picture of what was actually occurring until we combined the steps. It was such a great feeling of achievement each time we had a comprehensive grasp of the entire concept. We can apply the same process to reach a complete understanding of the steps necessary to achieve salvation. Working through each step separately, and then grasping the whole course, helps one envision the joy of being saved. God, by His mercy, ensures you a place in His Kingdom with Him; with our Lord and Savior, Jesus Christ; with the Theotokos; and with the important people in your life that you will join at the Last Judgment.

"Works" According to St. Paul

Paul uses the term "works" extensively in his letters, especially in Romans, Galatians, and Ephesians. By this term he means:

(1) *Dead Works:* These are evil works, such as murder, adultery, idol worshiping, robbery, and so on. In addition, dead works can be good works done for the wrong reasons. These are works like fasting, giving money, and feeding the poor done for the wrong reasons, such as to call attention to oneself or to gain standing in the community. Selfish motivation turns good works into dead works. The solution is not to cease fasting, giving, or helping, but to turn from the sin of self-glorification.

(2) *Living Works:* These are deeds that are both good in themselves and done for righteous purpose—to glorify God. Paul teaches that good works are an outgrowth of salvation when he writes, "For we are His workmanship, created in Christ Jesus for good works, which God has prepared beforehand that we should walk in them" (Eph. 2:10). Good works contribute to our faith as James teaches: "You see then that a man is justified by works, and not by faith only (or alone)" (James 2:24).

Some have misunderstood Paul, particularly in Romans 4, by interpreting that he meant to condemn all works. A careful reading of Romans, however, reveals that Paul is not putting down works in general, but *only dead works or works of the old Jewish law.* Thus, the Christian actively cultivates a habit of doing *good works* for the glory of God and as a way of life. If we are joined to Christ and cleansed from the dishonor of the past, we become "a vessel for honor, sanctified and useful for the Master, prepared for every good work" (2 Tim. 2:21). God sets us apart to Himself so we will be productive and useful to Him.

From Justification to Salvation

What is the transition from justification to salvation? We are first "justified by faith" and then "empowered by God for good works and deeds of righteousness." Orthodoxy believes one has to acquire faith then become righteous so that he can do good works. In essence, one follows the other. However, we do not discuss the one *versus* the other, as we look at them as a total unit. We believe that they are in union with one another; one cannot exist without the other in order to achieve salvation.

It is up to us to commit to and acquire faith through God's mercy, so that we will see the need and have the will to do good works and deeds of righteousness, in the hope we will obtain God's final grace at the Last Judgment. Good works is *"a necessary consequence of a faith-filled heart,"* but it is only part of the requirement of salvation. One cannot skip from justification of a faith-filled heart directly to the final step of being saved without performing good works and deeds of righteousness. The two are intimately linked, which allows believers to be assured of salvation through a changed heart and changed actions.

Chapter 10
READING THE HOLY BIBLE

What Is the Bible?

The Bible is God's book. Whenever we pick up His book—the Holy Bible—we are hearing the voice of the Master of the universe announcing His commandments to us. When we accept His words by faith and live by them, good things start to happen. Life changes, and it is continually transformed. Through the Bible, God's sayings offer a blueprint for life. The Bible contains letters of love from God to us and expresses His earnest longing for reconciliation, fellowship, and union with us.

The Liturgy itself is nothing but a recapitulation, true and living, making present again the events of the Bible itself. The hymns, the icons, the prayers, the readings all serve to convey to us the living message of the Bible. It is the cradle in which we find Christ today. He is the central figure and actor of the Bible. It is not Eve, the first sinner; not David, the adulterer; nor Solomon, the polygamist; nor Judas, the betrayer; nor Pilate, the crucifier; nor Peter, the denier; nor Paul, the persecutor turned preacher. Christ is always at the center.

The purpose of the Holy Scriptures is stated in John 20:31: "These things are written that you may believe that Jesus is the Christ, the Son of God, and that believing you may have life in His name." The intention of the Bible is not to teach historical or scientific facts, but theology and spiritual truths about God and man—to reveal God and His will to us. It is in the Bible that we find His promise and the record of His love.

Interpreting the Bible

The Orthodox Church upholds a great respect for the Bible as God's word. In fact, the holy fathers viewed the Bible as *an icon full of grace*. The Church, however, does not venerate the text of Scripture as if every word in the Bible was dictated by God verbatim and then written down word for word by the person who wrote each book. The Church does, however, believe that the persons writing each book were truly guided by the Holy Spirit. Thus, readers need a true interpreter of the Bible.

The Holy Spirit has been abiding in the Church since the day of Pentecost, guiding it to all truth. It was the early Church which established conclusively, under the guidance of the Holy Spirit, exactly which of the many books in circulation at that time were to be regarded as genuinely inspired by God and reflect His authentic revelation. The Church, then, is truly the divinely inspired interpreter of the Bible—not as truth itself, but as a record of truth.

Included below are various selected Bible events as examples of this record of truth, which include: the baptism of Jesus and His triumph over Satan; the Beatitudes, or blessings segment of the Sermon on the Mount; and selected miracles of Jesus. The church's interpretations, which were obtained from the Orthodox Study Bible (13), are also given for each Bible passage. Some of these events are also discussed in Chapter 4.

Matthew 3:13–4:10: The Baptism of Jesus; Jesus's Triumph Over Satan

Then Jesus came from Galilee to John at the Jordan to be baptized by him. And John tried to prevent Him, saying, "I need to be baptized by you, and are You coming to me?" But Jesus answered and said to him, *"Permit it to be so now, for thus it is fitting for us to fulfill all righteousness."* When He had been baptized, Jesus came up immediately from the water; and behold, the heavens were opened to Him, and He saw the Spirit of God descending like a dove, and alighting upon Him. And suddenly a voice came from heaven saying, "This is My beloved Son, in Whom I am well pleased."

Then Jesus was led up by the Spirit into the wilderness to be tempted by the devil. And when He had fasted forty days and forty nights, afterward He was hungry. Now when the tempter came to Him, he said, "If You are the Son of God, command that these stones become bread." But He answered and said, *"It is written, Man shall not live by bread alone, but by every word that precedes from the mouth of God."* Then the devil took Him up into the Holy City, set Him on the pinnacle of the temple and said to Him, "If You are the Son of God, throw Yourself down." Jesus said to him, *"It is written again, you shall not tempt the Lord your God."* Again the devil took Him up on an exceedingly high mountain, and showed Him all the kingdoms of the world and their glory. And he said to Him, "All these things I will give You if You will fall down and worship me." Then Jesus said to him, *"Away with you, Satan! For it is written you shall worship the Lord your God, and Him only you shall serve."*

Church Interpretation:

John the Baptist stated: "I need to be baptized by you, and are You coming to me?" Now, Jesus did not need purification through baptism. But by making the purification of humanity His own, He would wash away the sin of humanity, grant regeneration, and reveal the mystery of the Holy Trinity. Thus the baptism was necessary for the fulfillment of all of God's righteousness. St. Gregory of Nyssa says, "Jesus enters the filthy (sinful) waters of the world and when He comes out, brings up (purifies) the entire world with Him."

The Spirit of God hovered over the first creation in Genesis 1:2. After Jesus's baptism, the Holy Spirit comes in the form of a dove to anoint the Messiah, the Son of God, at the beginning of the new creation. Jesus, the eternal Son of God, did not become the Son of God on this day; rather, in His baptism the eternal Son of God is revealed to all humanity. The voice from heaven claims, "This is My beloved Son, in whom I am well pleased," thus revealing the deity of Christ, the naturally and begotten Son of God. The baptism of Jesus also reveals the great mystery of the Holy Spirit. The Father speaks; the Holy Trinity descends; the incarnate Son is baptized.

Jesus's humanity is best revealed through His interaction with Satan. Jesus was led to Satan so that He may be tempted in fundamental areas of faith. He went into the wilderness after His baptism to be tested by a struggle with the devil. We who are baptized into Him need not be defeated when temptations come along because, like Jesus, we are aided by the Holy Spirit. Jesus fasted for forty days to overcome temptation, giving us an example of our own power and our limitations. The hunger of the flesh does not control Him; rather, He controls His flesh. His fasting is the foundation of the church's forty-day Lenten observance before Holy Week, and also the fast before Christmas and Epiphany feasts. It is a spiritual preparation for the Passion and resurrection of Christ.

The devil challenges Jesus's relationship to the Father. "If You are the Son of God" calls into question the Father's declaration of Jesus's son-ship at His baptism (Matt. 3:17). The devil wants Jesus to abuse His divine powers, to act independently, detaching His own will of the Father. In His divine nature, the Son shares one will with the Father and the Spirit. But in His humanity He possesses "free will" and at all times must choose to remain in communion with His Father, to be obedient to the divine will. By rejecting the first temptation, Jesus rejects a kingdom based on materialism and earthly well-being—the "bread" which perishes. He teaches us not to love ease and comfort, but to accept willingly the struggle necessary to purify us from evil.

When the devil challenged Jesus to throw Himself down from the pinnacle of the temple, he puts God's power of protection to the test. Will Jesus depend on spectacular signs of self-aggrandizement, or will He humbly submit to persecution, humiliation, and death according to the Father's will? Jesus's answer, *You shall not tempt the Lord your God,* reveals that God's Kingdom is not one of earthly spectacle and fame. Therefore, we should never expose ourselves to danger just to test whether God is going to "protect" us. To do so is to *"tempt the Lord."*

Again the devil took Him up to an exceedingly high mountain and showed Him, and offered Him, the kingdom of the world. Jesus was offered a choice of worldly power over the Kingdom of God. The devil is "the ruler of this world" (John 12:31) "because the whole world is in his power" (1 John 5:19). Jesus refuses to take a road that would lead Him away from the path of suffering and death for the redemption of the world. Jesus says a simple command: *"Away with you, Satan."*

Matthew 5:1–12: Sermon on the Mount –The Beatitudes; The Blessings of True Discipleship

In the Sermon on the Mount, Jesus introduces the kind of life those seeking the Kingdom of God must lead. There are four different parts to it: (1) The Beatitudes, or Blessings; (2) The New Covenant; (3) Spiritual Disciplines; (4) Exhortation to Righteousness. (See Matthew 5:1–7:29; also see previous notes in Chapter 4.) This discussion includes the first part, the Beatitudes. Christ's sermon begins with the Beatitudes (the blessings) describing the joys of true discipleship, the blessed way of life. The people await the rewards Jesus's promises. In this case, the **Church Interpretations** are given with each individual blessing.

Matthew 5:3: *"Blessed are the poor in spirit, for theirs is the kingdom of heaven."*

Church Interpretation: "Blessed" in this context indicates heavenly, spiritual blessedness, rather than earthly happiness or prosperity. In Hebrew, "poor" means both (1) the materially poor and (2) the faithful among God's people. "The poor in spirit" and the humble and lowly have the heart of the poor and their total dependence upon God. These are truly the spiritually rich.

Matthew 5:4: *"Blessed are those who mourn, for they shall be comforted."*

Church Interpretation: By means of holy sorrow, we can keep watch over our hearts and learn self-control. *"Those who mourn"* over their sins and the suffering of mankind in the new age are genuinely repentant and will "*be comforted*" in the new age. Holy sorrow is part of conversion, the consummation of repentance, and the first fruit of infinite joy. It is distinguished from ungodly sorrow, a sadness that leads to despair (see 2 Cor. 7:10).

Matthew 5:5: "*Blessed are the meek, for they shall inherit the earth.*"

Church Interpretation: Mourning can extinguish the flame of anger and make a person "*meek.*" Meekness is an attitude of being content with both honor and dishonor. It is an imitation of Christ who said, "*Learn from Me, for I am gentle (meek) and lowly in heart*" (Matt. 11:29). The meek are God-controlled, and through their prayers God gives them mastery over their passions—especially anger. Meekness is not passive gentleness, but strength under control. Jesus's promise of future blessings is not for the powerful, the rich, and the violent, but for those who are meek and humble: "*They shall inherit the earth,*" the new earth, which is everlasting.

Matthew 5:6: "*Blessed are those who hunger and thirst for righteousness, for they shall be filled.*"

Church Interpretation: "*Those who hunger and thirst for righteousness*"—such followers who are justified see the presence of God and His Kingdom as the most important thing in their lives.

Matthew 5:7: "*Blessed are the merciful, for they shall obtain mercy.*"

Church Interpretation: "*Mercy*" is love set in motion, love expressed in action, God's loving kindness. His mercy took our suffering upon Himself in order to grant us His kingdom, which sets us free from captivity to the evil one. In view of God's loving kindness, we in turn are to be merciful to all others.

Matthew 5:8: "*Blessed are the pure in heart, for they shall see God.*"

Church Interpretation: To be pure is to be unmixed with anyone else. The *"pure in heart"* are devoted to the worship and service of God. With the aid of the Holy Spirit (1) they practice all virtue, (2) they are not conscious of any evil in themselves, and (3) they live in temperance—a stage of spirituality attained by few in this life. When the soul is not dominated by sinful passions or its energy dissipated by the things of this world, its only desire is God. Then the heart, holding fast to the new life in Christ and contemplating the glory of God, *"shall see God* through communion with His Son"* (2 Cor. 3:18).

Matthew 5:9: *"Blessed are the peacemakers, for they shall be called sons of God."*

Church Interpretation: Being Himself the source of peace, the Son of God found no price sufficient for peace but that of shedding His own blood. In doing so, Christ reveals Himself to us as the Reconciler, the Prince of Peace (Isaiah 9:6; Eph. 2:14, 16). The Holy Spirit gives peace, the sign of God's presence, to those who meditate on Christ and imitate Him. Peace brings communion with Christ and concord with all creation, which is the sign of sanctity. Thus *"peacemakers"* share God's peace with those around them, partaking in the work of God's Son and becoming by God's grace *"sons of God"* themselves.

Matthew 5:10: *"Blessed are those who are persecuted for righteousness' sake, for theirs is the kingdom of God."*

Church Interpretation: Children of God uphold God's truth and refuse to compromise with the way of the world. They give themselves to no other (Matt. 6:24, 33). It is not surprising then that they, like Jesus, should be *"persecuted for righteousness' sake."* For Christ's *"kingdom"* is the crown awaiting the righteous.

Matthew 5:11, 12: *"Blessed are you when they revile and persecute you, and say all kinds of evil against you falsely for My sake. Rejoice and be exceedingly glad, for great is your reward in heaven, for so they persecuted the prophets who were before you."*

Church Interpretation: In willingness to suffer persecution, the Christian shows his loyalty and unity with Jesus Christ. He walks the road of the prophets, saints, and martyrs. The Greek for *"exceedingly glad"* means to "leap exceedingly with joy." Suffering with Christ is attended with inexpressible joy.

The Miracles of Jesus:

Luke 8:22–25: The Miracle of Jesus Calming a Storm

Now it happened on a certain day, that He got into a boat with His disciples. And He said to them, *"Let us cross over to the other side of the lake."* And they launched out. But as they sailed He fell asleep. And a windstorm came down on the lake, and they were filling with water, and were in jeopardy. And they came to Him and awoke Him, saying, "Master, Master, we are perishing!" Then He awoke and rebuked the wind and the raging of the water. And they ceased and there was a calm. But He said to them, *"Where is your faith?"* And they were afraid, and marveled, saying to one another, "Who can this be? For He commands even the wind and the water, and they obey Him!"

Church Interpretation: In the most difficult moments of life, "*faith*" unites us with Christ and gives us His strength and comfort.

Luke 8:41–56: Miracles of the Daughter of Jairus Being Raised, and A Woman Healed

And behold, there came a man named Jairus, and he was a ruler of the synagogue. And he fell down at Jesus's feet and begged Him to come to his house, for he had an only daughter about twelve years of age, and she was dying. But as He went the multitudes thronged Him.

Now a woman, having a flow of blood for twelve years, who had spent all her livelihood on physicians and could not be healed by any, came from behind and touched the border of His garment. And immediately her flow of blood stopped. And He said *"Who touched Me?"* When all denied it, Peter and those with him said, "Master, the multitudes throng and press You." But Jesus said, *"Somebody touched Me, for I perceived power going out from Me."* Now when the woman saw that she was not hidden, she came trembling; and falling down before Him, she declared to Him in the presence of all the people the reason she had touched Him and how she was healed immediately. And He said to her, *"Daughter, be of good cheer; your faith has made you well. Go in peace."*

While He was still speaking, someone came from the ruler of the synagogue's house, saying to him. "Your daughter is dead. Do not trouble the teacher." But when Jesus heard it, He answered him saying, *"Do not be afraid; only believe and she will be made well."* When He came into the house, He permitted no one to go in except, Peter, James, and John, and the father and mother of the girl. Now all wept and mourned for her, but He said, *"Do not weep; she is not dead, but sleeping."* And they ridiculed Him, knowing that she was dead. But He put them outside, took her by the hand and called, saying, *"Little girl arise."* Then her spirit returned and she arose immediately. And He commanded that she be given something to eat. And her parents were astonished, but He charged them to tell no one what had happened.

Church Interpretation: Jairus, a leader of the synagogue, came to Jesus, even though at that point many of the leaders did not believe that Jesus was the Messiah. Yet they considered Him a threat to their power over the Jewish people. This insecurity is an indication that the spirit of Jesus is beginning to have a hold on the synagogue leaders and the multitudes who thronged Him. The masses were not asking Him to depart as did the throngs at Gadarene (Luke 8:26–39) when He commanded the demons to go from a man who was possessed into a herd of swine that ran into a lake and drowned. In the case of Gadarene, the multitude, thinking that Jesus was also a threat to their herds, asked Him to depart.

Healing power flows from Christ into the woman who touched Him. Despite her flow of blood for twelve years, that which Jesus touches, or which touches Him, is sanctified, and the woman was healed. Others may have touched Christ, but this woman's faith draws His power. The power to heal comes out of Jesus and flows through His garment. Similarly, we use physical things, like paint or wood of an icon, the metal of a cross, water or oil, if it is sanctified by Christ through faith and prayer.

Christ was not troubled when He was delayed on His way to Jairus's house by the healing of the woman, even though a person from his synagogue announced that Jairus's daughter was dead. Jesus knew that He had the divine power to raise her from the dead, so he exhorts the parents to *"only believe."* We are to believe God, even when it appears there is no hope. These parents do continue to believe, and their daughter is made well. Christ's divinity works together with His humanity to accomplish miracles. Here, taking the child by the hand and calling her to *"arise,"* is an action of His humanity. Her being restored to life is an action of His divinity. These two operations, however, are inseparable because He is one undivided Person.

Mark 8:1–9 – Jesus Feeding the Four Thousand

In those days, the multitude being very great and having nothing to eat, Jesus called His disciples to Him and said to them, *"I have compassion on the multitude, because they have now continued with Me three days and have nothing to eat .And if I send them away hungry to their own houses, they will faint on the way; for some of them have come from afar."* Then His disciples answered Him, "How can one satisfy these people with bread here in the wilderness?" He asked them, *"How many loaves do you have?"* And they said, "Seven." So He commanded the multitudes to sit down on the ground. And He took the seven loaves and gave thanks, broke them and gave them to His disciples to set before them; and they set them before the multitudes. They also had a few small fish; and having blessed them, He said to set them also before them. So they ate and were filled, and they took up seven large baskets of leftover fragments. Now those who had eaten were about four thousand. And He sent them away.

Church Interpretation: The miracle of the feeding of the four thousand, reported by Mark above and Mathew (15:32–39) shows Jesus feeding His people as God fed the Israelites in the desert. The Church Fathers see in this an image of the Eucharist, an idea also expressed in John 6, the discourse on the Bread of Life. This miracle is probably not a duplicate report of the first miracle of the feeding of the five thousand with five loaves and two fish, but another performed in a different place. The feeding of the four thousand includes many Gentiles and took place in the region of the Decapolis, southeast of the sea of Galilee. To feed the hungry in the wilderness is a messianic sign, fulfilling the prophecy, "Can God prepare a table in the wilderness? Can He give bread also?"

When He blessed the seven loaves and few fish, before He broke them and gave them to His disciples for distribution to the multitudes, Jesus is teaching us not to eat until we first give thanks to God. The terminology reminds us of the Last Supper (see Luke 22:15–20) and leads to the Eucharist interpretation of this miracle. The participation of the disciples in distributing the loaves and the fish is important. In the Church, Jesus feeds His flock at the Eucharist through His servants, the priests.

Summary

The above passages recounted major events in the ministry of Christ. The *Church Interpretations* of these passages show how these events relate to our everyday lives and how we should utilize the instructions and commands of our Lord and Savior, Jesus Christ, so that we may achieve eternal salvation. The above events are only an infinitesimal portion of the holy gospel; one can't imagine the magnitude of what we can receive if we read the complete Bible while at the same time applying the proper Church Interpretations.

Narrative of Selected Books in the New Testament

Accounts of selected books of the New Testament are illustrated below. After reading each narrative, you should read the actual book contained in the Bible. The explanations for each of the narratives included below have been obtained from The Orthodox Study

Bible: Discovering Orthodox Christianity in the pages of the New Testament and the Psalms (New King James Version) (15).

1. Matthew: The Gospel of St. Matthew is attributed to Matthew, identified as a tax collector and one of Jesus's twelve disciples. The book was likely written during the period between 50 and 70 AD. In this Gospel, Matthew identifies Christ as the incarnate God who has inaugurated the Kingdom of God and the New Covenant. He shows conclusively that Christ fulfills the prophecies of the Old Testament, establishes the New Covenant through His death and resurrection, and will continue to guide His Church to the end of the age. Jesus proclaims that God's reign has come as His Father's power is manifested in His Son, and that the fullness of the Kingdom will be consummated at Christ's Second Coming. St. Matthew depicts that the Person of Jesus, at once God and Man, radiates the immediacy of God's presence by His words and actions. He portrays Jesus as the great Teacher and Interpreter of God's law through His preaching of the Sermon on the Mount (5:1–7:29). St. Matthew describes the miracles of Jesus, which bear witness to His saving power, restoring health to creation and counteracting the deceits of Satan.

2. Mark: The Apostle Mark, also known as John Mark, is widely attested by the ancient Church as the author of this gospel. John Mark as a young man assisted Paul and Barnabas on their earliest missionary journeys. Later he also aided Peter and, according to tradition, mainly used Peter's teaching as his primary source for this gospel. St. Mark is the shortest of the gospels that features simplicity of language and a rapid pace of narration. By the end of the first chapter, Christ has been baptized and performed numerous miracles. Mark describes Christ as the "suffering Messiah" who has come to serve and give His life for many. Jesus is clearly the Son of God

who has power over demons, heals the sick, and forgives sins. But He also possesses full humanity, expressed through the agony of Gethsemane and the suffering on the cross. Mark underscores the fact that Jesus conceals His messianic identity in spite of His preaching and teaching, His miracles, His authority over evil spirits, and the forgiveness of sins He granted. In an effort to discourage popular political ideas about the Messiah from cropping up, Jesus commanded demons, the people He healed, and even the disciples to keep silent about His Messiah-ship until He chose to reveal the mystery before the Sanhedrin.

3. Luke: Luke was a Gentile from Antioch by birth, and a physician by profession. He was a fellow worker of Paul's. As was indicated in the Acts of the Apostles, Luke was with Paul as he traveled the coast of Asia Minor on the way to Jerusalem. Luke has been responsible for two New Testament books: the Gospel of St. Luke and the Acts of the Apostles. He probably wrote his gospel from Greece or from Asia Minor in 70 to 80 AD. Luke has been called a "historian" because his biblical events are historically dated chronologically. Luke starts with Jesus's birth and early life, and then proceeds through His baptism, His ministry, crucifixion, resurrection, and ascension. Since this is a gospel written for Christians of Gentile background, it emphasizes more than the other gospels the trials of missions and evangelization. Salvation is described as a "light to bring revelation to the Gentiles" (2:32). At the end of the gospel, the risen Lord instructs His disciples to preach repentance and the forgiveness of sins "*to all nations*" (24:47). Three aspects of the Christian life are emphasized throughout Luke, perhaps revealing the author's own spiritual gifts and strengths. These are:

    1. *Prayer:* The early chapters elevate the examples of righteous men and women offering gifts, hymns,

and prayers to God. Jesus is portrayed frequently at prayer, especially before every important step in His ministry. The gospel ends with the disciples "continually in the temple praising and blessing God" (24:53).

2. *The Activity of the Holy Spirit:* The inspirational work of the Holy Spirit is everywhere evident in the Gospel of Luke. Mary is "overshadowed" by the Spirit (1:35). The spirit leads Zacharias to prophecy (1:67). Jesus conducts His ministry in the fullness of the Spirit (3:22; 4:1, 18; 10:21). The disciples were to embark upon their world mission after receiving "power from on high" (24:49), the gift of the Spirit.

3. *A Deep Concern for Sinners:* Luke reports throughout his gospel Jesus's concern and love for sinners, with a confidant hope of their repentance and forgiveness.

4. John: According to tradition, St. John the Apostle was assisted by St. Prochoros in writing this gospel. John, called "son of thunder" (Mark 3:17), was one of the twelve apostles of Jesus. John and his brother, the Apostle James, were fisherman by trade like their father Zebedee. John is believed to be the youngest apostle and also the "beloved disciple" of Christ (13:23; 21:7, 20). John was a pillar of the Church in Jerusalem, and later moved to Ephesus. He served as the leading authority of Ephesus for the remainder of his ministry. John was exiled to the island of Patmos from 81–96 AD where he wrote Revelation. He then returned to Ephesus upon the death of the Roman emperor and wrote his gospel. Because of his insight and deep thought evident in his gospel, which has been called "the Spiritual Gospel," John was named by the Church as "the Theologian." The New Testament contains four other books, in addition to his gospel, attributed to John—three letters, written

around 90 AD, and the Book of Revelation, written in 95 AD. The Gospel of John, written in 96 AD, is considered the last of the four gospels to be written. St. John the Apostle died shortly after the completion of this gospel at almost one hundred years old. John's major theme is that the eternal Son of God has come in the flesh. The gospel was written "that you may believe that Jesus is the Christ, the Son of God, and that believing you may have life in His name" (20:31). The Gospel of John has many other theological themes, which include the following:

1. *The Trinity:* God the Father is the Unbegotten and is the source of the Son. The Son has one and the same nature as the Father and is the only Begotten of the Father. The Holy Spirit is distinguished from the Father in person, proceeding from Him. The Father sent both the Son and the Holy Spirit.

2. *Glory:* Glorification is the prominent theme in John's theology. The glory of God is manifested in Christ's earthly ministry, but the Church in the power of the Holy Spirit also experiences His glory. Glorification begins not in the next life, but now, commencing with the incarnation of Christ and continuing with those who receive a new birth. In John:

   a) We behold Christ's glory through the incarnation (1:14).

   b) Jesus manifests His glory to us so we might believe (2:11; 11:40).

   c) Jesus seeks glory for the Father (7:18), but not for Himself (8:50).

   d) The Father's glory is given to us by the Son (17:22).

   e) We will behold God's glory when we are with Him in eternity (17:24).

3. *The Spiritual Dimension:* John's gospel is not strictly historical. This is also a "spiritual gospel" because

the mystical, theological perspective dominates and is reflected to this day in the theology and liturgical practices of the Orthodox Church. Everything in life is conditioned by the realm and activity of God the Trinity, whose eternal glory, life, and light is shared with those who believe.

4. *The Sacramental Dimension:* A sacrament is an event in which God's grace works together with our faith to bring us into closer communion with Him. The sacraments are called "mysteries" (Gr. *mystirion*), for by them God, through the action of grace, bestows divine life on all who live by faith and obedience, a foretaste of the fulfillment of salvation in the age to come. In the Gospel of John, there are direct references, as well as many citations, to the sacraments:

   a) *Baptism:* As water is a necessity of life, so the water of baptism, together with the Holy Spirit, is necessary for eternal life, thus fulfilling Isaiah's prophecy that God's people will joyfully draw water from the wells of salvation (Is. 12:3; 58:11).

   b) *Anointing by the Spirit (chrismation):* In the Gospel of John, it is difficult to distinguish a baptismal reference from a chrismational one. Jesus speaks to Nicodemus about "water and the Spirit" (3:5). To the Samaritan woman He promises the gift of "living water" (4:10, 14), which the evangelist himself interprets as new life by the gift of the Spirit (7:38, 39).

   c) *The Eucharist:* The Church Fathers found allusions to the Eucharist in the wine at Cana and the bread for feeding the five thousand, an event which provided the setting for Jesus's discourse on the bread of life. Certainly 6:52– 59 (the command to *eat His flesh, drink His blood)* is a powerful biblical expression of the sacramental and eucharistic basis for Christian life. In this passage, Christ speaks not merely of eating the bread of life through faith alone, but of the eating of His flesh and the drinking of His blood—which can only refer to the Eucharist as a mystical, sacramental act uniting us with Him.

5. *The Church:* The Gospel of John testifies to a strong sense of community among the disciples. In John's perspective, the Divine Word, the Son of God, came into the world to save the world and, through the life of the Church, to offer the whole world up to God. Christ and His Church instigate this transformation.

5. Acts of the Apostles: Acts is a continuation by Luke, the beloved physician, of the account given in his gospel. It was written between 75 and 85 AD. In this book Luke, describes the spread of the gospel by the apostles, from Jerusalem to the whole world (1:8). The Book of Acts recounts the triumphant march of the Christian mission from Jerusalem to Samaria, Syria, Cyprus, Asia Minor, Greece, and finally Rome, the capital of the empire. This achievement points to the work of the Holy Spirit, who descended on the early Church, empowering the apostles and other missionaries to bring the good news of salvation to the known world. Acts moves from the ascension of the Lord (1:9), through the first meeting of the twelve and the 120 for prayer (1:12–15), to the labors and lessons of Peter (1:15–6:7), the conversion and missionary journeys of Paul (7:58–28:31), and lastly to the rapid spread of the Church throughout the Mediterranean world (9:31–21:14). Chapters 1–12 focus largely on the ministry of Peter, while chapters 13–28 concentrate exclusively on Paul. With Peter we see the Church being established. With Paul we see

the expansion of the Church throughout the Roman world.

6. Paul's Epistle to the Romans: St. Paul wrote his epistle to the Romans in 55–57 AD during the latter part of Paul's third missionary journey (referenced in Acts 20:3–21:16), most likely while he was in Corinth. His major theme illustrates God's righteousness revealed in Christ for our salvation (1:16, 17). Righteousness is the basis of a faithful relationship between God and humanity. God freely offers this living and growing relationship to all through Christ. Other themes include:
   1. The natural mortality and actual sinfulness of all (1:18–3:20)
   2. Salvation through Christ apart from the Mosaic law (3:21–4:25); we live by faith in response to grace, rather than by the dead works of the law
   3. New life in Christ; freedom from sin, death, and the law through our sacramental identity with Christ, established in holy baptism (chapters 5–7)
   4. New life in the Holy Spirit; the power to be God-like, established in chrismation (chapter 8)
   5. God's plan for Jews and Gentiles, and their reconciliation in Christ (chapters 9–11)
   6. Christian life in the Church and in the world (chapters 12–16)

In Romans and Galatians, Paul deals extensively with the relation of the Old Covenant to belief in Christ, and how Gentiles can be full members of the New Covenant by grace through faith and good works. Romans has several qualities that set it apart from the rest of Paul's epistles: Romans is Paul's most significant letter; it summarizes the entire gospel; and Romans is Paul's most logical letter. It is the only letter Paul wrote to a church he had not yet visited. Paul was hoping to obtain Rome's support for his planned mission to Rome and Spain (15:24, 28, 29). While most of Paul's epistles correct doctrinal or moral problems, Romans proclaims the faith more completely and systematically, addressing few specific problems.

7. Paul's First and Second Epistles to the Corinthians: A theme resonates in the letters to the Church at Corinth—we are created for communion with God and with each other. Here Paul espouses Christian morality and Church discipline. There was Church disunity there as many of the Corinthian Christians had broken into several factions and the Church became spiritually weak and succumbed to the moral failure for which the city was famous. Paul also touches on many other important theological issues, emphasizing reconciliation and communion with God and with each other.

8. Paul's Epistle to the Galatians: As he did in Romans, Paul deals extensively with the relation of the Old Covenant to belief in Christ, and how Gentiles can be full members of the New Covenant by grace through faith and good works (the true gospel versus the false gospel). After initially believing in the gospel of Jesus Christ as a gift of God, many of the Christians in Galatia had turned to the teaching of the Jewish legal law. Paul's view is that spiritual discipline is not bondage; rather it is a rejection of bondage, a pursuit of holiness while gaining freedom from *legalism (the old Jewish law)* and sinful passions. Paul discusses the gift of the Holy Spirit, the cross of Christ, and the life of faith.

9. Paul's Epistle to the Ephesians: To the Church of Ephesus Paul discusses the riches of Christ in the Church. The mystery of salvation in the Church, which is the Body of Christ, is not only for all mankind, but it is for all creation, affecting this age and the age to come. The *Body of Christ* is the center and life of all. Paul emphasizes sacramental theology of the church: the Holy Trinity and the sacraments of the Church, alluding to baptism, chrismation, the Eucharist, and marriage. His discourse

on marriage is the epistle reading for the Orthodox Christian wedding ceremony.

10. Paul's Epistle to the Colossians: The primary purpose of this epistle was to combat a form of Gnosticism—the blend of Jewish and Oriental ideas—which was taking hold in the Colossian church. The heretics causing this thought they were supplementing apostolic Christianity, which they saw as primitive, with greater knowledge. Paul's strategy to show how the heretics were distorting the truth was by way of apostolic tradition within the Church, which teaches that Christ alone is the Lord and He alone is sufficient. True spirituality is life in Christ in the apostolic Church. Through Christ's incarnation, Passion, and resurrection, which we join Him in by means of baptism and grow into Him through transformation of life, we have direct access to God's fullness. The Church, the Body of Christ, is the new creation, and through the Church all creation will be renewed.

11. Paul's First Epistle to the Thessalonians: First Thessalonians was written in Corinth in 50–51 AD. The church in Thessalonica was established in the summer of 50 AD during Paul's second missionary journey. While many of the early churches were composed primarily of Jews who believed in Christ, the Thessalonian believers were mostly Gentiles who were former idol worshipers. First Thessalonians is probably the first of Paul's New Testament epistles, and perhaps the first of all the twenty-seven New Testament books written. When Paul left Thessalonica, the new church was exemplary (1:3, 7–10; 4:9, 10) but young and unstable. A few months later, while Paul was in Athens (3:1), he grew concerned about how the Thessalonian church handled persecution by fellow citizens, stirred up by the Jews (1:6; 2:14; Acts 17:5–9). He sent Timothy to encourage the faithful and return with a report. Subsequently, Timothy met Paul

in Corinth and presented the report. Paul's purpose in 1 Thessalonians is to respond to Timothy's report, correct the Thessalonians in their response, and encourage them to greater spiritual excellence. Paul encourages the Thessalonians to be holy because a holy life leads to eternal life. Paul emphasizes in particular: (1) continue as examples to others (1:7); (2) walk worthy of God's calling (2:12); (3) stand fast in the faith (3:8); and (4) maintain moral purity (4:3). The letter closes with instruction and comfort concerning the Second Coming of Christ (4:13–5:11), along with other exhortations concerning spiritual life.

12. Paul's Second Epistle to the Thessalonians: This epistle was written by Paul in Corinth in 51 AD. Timothy and Silas, who helped in establishing the church at Thessalonica, contributed to 2 Thessalonians. A few months after writing 1 Thessalonians, Paul received another report from Timothy. The Thessalonian Christians' faith, amid persecution by the Roman Empire, stood firm. Second Thessalonians was written approximately twenty years after the ascension, and already people were speculating on the Lord's return. Hearsay concerning the Second Coming of Christ was increasing. Some of the Thessalonians had been shaken in the faith by conjecture on Christ's return; some even said that the day of the Lord had already come. Others grew so excited about the end times that they abandoned their jobs and lived off the charity of the Church. Still others grew desponded and wavered in hope. Paul had taught that signs precede the Second Coming of the Lord and that we did not have the capacity to predict the time. So he wrote this letter: (a) to encourage further endurance in persecution, (b) to correct mistaken ideas concerning the Second Coming of Christ and improper lifestyles arising from these ideas, and (c) to offer assurance that his teaching is apostolic (2:15).

13. **Paul's First Epistle to Timothy:** This epistle to Timothy appears to have been written in 64–65 AD, before Paul's second imprisonment in Rome, perhaps while in Macedonia. First Timothy is both personal and pastoral. Whereas most of Paul's letters are addressed to the Church in a particular location, the pastoral epistles are written to instruct specific leaders—in this case Timothy, Bishop of Ephesus. A pastoral epistle was also written to Titus, Bishop of Crete. Paul speaks as an experienced mentor instructing his students, his "sons" as apostles and bishops. Regarding the epistle to Timothy, the major theme is the pastoral care of the faithful; the Church is to manifest the Kingdom of God on earth. Therefore, the government of the Church is integrally connected with both apostolic doctrine (1:1–20; 3:14–4:5) and worship (2:1–15). Paul writes to guide Timothy as he encounters pastoral challenges and questions. To accomplish this Paul includes the following:

1. Paul opposes false doctrine with apostolic doctrine, showing that the world is not inherently evil (it is sin that is evil) but good, for God created the world; salvation is not by knowledge, but by faith, which calls people out of their sinful state (1:15; 2:3–6); Jesus Christ is at once fully God and fully man (2:5, 6), sharing fully our humanity (3:16; 6:13).

2. Paul opposes false leaders by upholding godly apostolic leaders (1:12–20; 3:1–16), especially Timothy, who had long been one of Paul's chosen missionaries and who had accompanied him on several of his missionary journeys.

3. Paul sets up administrative guidelines for the Church, making it clear there must be no hostility between the institutional element or structure of the Church and the charismatic element of the Church energized by the Spirit. Paul uses a good portion of

this pastoral epistle to provide *spiritual direction.* Paul's pastoral epistles hold unparalleled insight into the historical workings of the early Church as guided by the Holy Spirit; they are a foundational source for pastoral theology, for clergy and their relationship to the Church.

14. Paul's Epistle to Titus: Titus was a Gentile converted to Christ by St. Paul (1:4). The circumstances, content, and organization of the epistle to Titus are similar to 1 Timothy. The two epistles were probably written about the same time, in 63–65 AD. Timothy and Titus have extraordinary assignments. They are responsible for several communities (1:5), and they take part with the presbytery in ordinations (1 Tim. 5:22) while bringing unity to the presbyters (1 Tim. 5:17–22). The original apostles repeatedly faced death and passed on their apostolic authority to a new generation of Church leaders. Toward the end of Paul's third missionary journey, about 57 AD, Titus was sent from Ephesus to Corinth to resolve some problems occurring at that church. He restored the Corinthian church to proper order and reported back to Paul. Shortly thereafter, Paul sent Titus back to Corinth to deliver the letter we call 2 Corinthians (2 Cor. 8:16, 17; 12:18). After Paul was released from prison in Rome, about 63 AD, he and Titus visited Crete (1:5). When Paul moved on, he appointed Titus as apostolic overseer of Crete. According to tradition, Titus became Bishop of Crete and died there in old age. Paul's epistle to Titus confronted the theological problems in Crete similar to those faced by Timothy in Asia Minor. Paul here advises Titus on overseeing the Church according to the true faith. As the Church grew, it naturally developed theology and structure, later encountering heresy and sub-Christian behavior among its members. Paul here advises Titus as he faces these issues.

15. Paul's Epistle to the Hebrews: In the early centuries of the Church, several differing opinions circulated as to the

authorship of Hebrews. By the fourth century most Church authorities ascribed Hebrews to St. Paul, including St. John Chrysostom and St. Athanasius. The Council at Carthage (397 AD) canonized Hebrews as one of the fourteen epistles of Paul. Although all Orthodox lectionaries introduce Hebrews as being the epistle of the holy Apostle Paul to the Hebrews, many biblical scholars today contend that the authorship of this letter is uncertain. Hebrews seems to be written to Greek-speaking Jewish Christians, perhaps in Palestine, who were being drawn back to Judaism. Thus, the major emphasis is that Jesus Christ, the incarnate Son, is superior to the prophets, angels, Moses, and Aaron. Jesus offers a better priesthood, sanctuary, and sacrifice, for in worshiping Him we enter heaven. Therefore, we must faithfully hold fast to Him. Hebrews also includes: (a) the superiority of Christ and His sacrifice over Judaism, and (b) encouragement to continue in the Christian faith. Hebrews is not primarily a theological treatise but a rescue operation, a "word of exhortation" (13:22) to hold fast to the faith and persevere (3:6, 14; 10:23, 35–39; 12:1, 2). Nevertheless, Hebrews serves as one of the earliest dissertations on the doctrine of Christ. It reveals that Jesus Christ is the Son of God and what He has done, is doing, and will do forever in His earthly and heavenly ministry. Hebrews also serves as a treatise on Christian liturgical theology. It shows how the New Covenant fulfills and perfects Old Covenant Liturgy, and how New Covenant worship enters into heaven itself. For in the Eucharist, we participate in Christ's once-for-all sacrifice (9:26–28). It is He who offers and is offered. As Christ enters into heaven bodily in His full human nature, so do we. As we come to know Christ and His work for us, we must stand firm and never reject God's grace. The Christian life is one of faith, love, and good works.

16. The Epistle of James: Early Church tradition ascribes this letter to James, the "brother" or kinsman, of our Lord , known as James the Just. His main theme in this epistle is

the harmony of faith and works. The letter has many direct parallels with the Sermon on the Mount. James does not teach that we are saved by works, but he does teach that a dead faith, one without works, does not save. This is an early dissertation against invisible religion, wherein salvation by faith does not require visible works. James refutes the teaching that moral behavior is irrelevant to salvation. James is clear on these points: the human will is not bypassed in salvation; and grace does not nullify personal responsibility. The apostles made James the first bishop of Jerusalem. (Acts 12:17; 21:17, 18; Gal. 1:18, 19; 2:9), where he presided over the first Council of the Apostles at Jerusalem in 50 AD (Acts 15:13). James was the ideal bishop for Jerusalem, for he lived a strict and holy life, praying frequently in the temple. The Jews considered him incorruptible, for he obeyed the Law of Moses better than they. And they found no fault with him, except he confessed Jesus to be the Messiah. James argues that "works" (meaning Jewish deeds of formal, legalistic obedience) do not earn salvation. The root problem is solved by God's grace received by faith through the belief and acceptance of His Son, Jesus Christ. He upholds "works" meaning willed actions flowing from belief as the life of true evangelical faith. Both Paul and James distinguish between faith and works—sometimes differing in emphasis and vocabulary—but they never separate them! For faith coupled with works forms a living unity, a singular reality, which is true Christianity. Unlike most New Testament letters, James does not address a particular church or geographical region. Rather he addresses "the twelve tribes which are scattered abroad" (1:1). The letter was written in elegant Greek, and there is no indication that it addresses only Jewish Christians. Furthermore, James emphasizes that the New Testament identifies the whole Church as the New Israel (Gal. 6:15; Phil. 3:3; 1 Pet. 1:1; Rev. 7:4–8). The people James addresses are experiencing various trials: persecution, economic injustice and poverty, deception, and divisions among the Church. In response to these trials, the people are tempted by depression, anger, bitterness, and impatience. But they are plagued most by the classic sin of hypocrisy—the cleavage between faith and works, which is manifested in distrust, dissension, and quarrels. James uses his authority as bishop for spiritual discipline. He concentrates on rekindling true living faith and on the practice of repentance, trust, humility, patience, and self-control. The epistle of James could be called "New Testament wisdom literature." It is more a sermon than a letter, rephrasing sayings both from the Jewish wisdom tradition and from Jesus. The letter is a Christian handbook on ethics and it is most often quoted in the spiritual and theological writings of the Church in affirming the completion of faith by works. According to tradition, James was executed at the prompting of the Sanhedrin in 62 AD, being thrown from the temple walls and then clubbed to death. October 23 is the remembrance of his martyrdom.

17. The First and Second Epistles of Peter: After Peter had helped to establish the church in Antioch, he preached the gospel to Jews and Gentile converts to Judaism throughout northern Asia Minor (1 Peter 1:1). Later in Rome, upon hearing that the churches of Asia Minor were being persecuted, he wrote them a letter of encouragement. The first letter of Peter emphasizes to rejoice in sharing the sufferings of Christ. It is an exhortation for Christians suffering persecution to remember and live in their baptism into the life of Christ. Peter teaches that as baptism is a death and a resurrection, so Christians must enter into unjust suffering with a spirit of death and resurrection. Indeed, every trouble of life can be entered into as a baptismal experience, an ongoing acceptance of death in this life in order to grow in the qualities of the life to come. Our goal is the fulfillment of baptism (going to heaven) for through the resurrection reality of baptism, our true and eternal homeland is the Kingdom of God. Attaining this goal requires unwavering commitment in this

life to: (1) holiness (1 Peter 1:3–2:10), (2) submission in the roles we have in life (1 Peter 2:11–3:12), (3) patient suffering in this age as we wait for the age to come (1 Peter 3:13–4:19), and (4) disciplined unity in the church (1 Peter 15:1–11). The wide range of dispersion that Peter speaks has never been determined. After the martyrdom of Stephen (33 AD), many Christians fled from persecution in Jerusalem. Accordingly, some fled after the martyrdom of James the Just, Bishop of Jerusalem, in 62 AD. Some theologians speculate that Peter is speaking more generally of Christians at large, who were often ill treated and forced into exile because of their faith. It is believed that Peter wrote his second epistle during his imprisonment in Rome (63–67). In his second epistle, he emphasizes true knowledge versus false knowledge. Though the world disbelieves, deceives, and mocks, Christians must maintain apostolic doctrine and the Christian way of life. "We are to grow continually in holiness and virtue and pursue an entrance into the everlasting kingdom" (2 Peter 1:11), which is to come. Following the writing of the second epistle, tradition claims Peter was martyred in Rome during Nero's reign around 67 AD.

18. The First, Second, and Third Epistles of John: The first epistle's similarity to John's gospel and the apparent age of its author suggest it was written at a time late in John's life, about the same time as he wrote his gospel (90–95 AD). The major theme is a test of true Christian life. Jesus Christ, the incarnate God, reveals the light (1 John 1:5–7), love (1 John 4:7–11), and life (1 John 5:11–13) of the Father, as contrasted with the darkness (1 John 1:6), hatred (1 John 2:9–11), and death (1 John 5:12) of the present world. Thus, John can be read as a commentary on the reality of baptism, chrismation, and the Eucharist in our lives. Inclusive would be: our participation or communion with God and with each other; the close relationship of faith, love, obedience, and life— the all-inclusive term for salvation; the close relationship between the first great commandment, love of God, and

the second, love of others—especially of fellow Christians; and the crucial importance of holding true faith. First John is mostly pastoral and positive, written to protect 'God's people. Living the truth is the best argument against what is false. A teacher of Christian religion and morals is one who lives in God, knows God, and therefore does what is true. John is against: false teachers who used Christian words with redefined meanings and who sound orthodox without being so, and former members of the Church who had left and decried the Church, her sacraments, and her theology, and were a threat to the faith of Christians. The second and third epistles of John suggest a date of composition close to John's gospel and 1 John. Second John emphasizes that the love of our incarnate God brings promised victory over the Antichrist. It warns that deceivers are heretics, as evidenced by their denial of the incarnation of the Son of God. The third epistle of John exhorts the Church to persevere in the true faith, which she has received. True Christian leaders will adhere to that faith and respect those who passed the truth on to them. John especially notes the traditions concerning the incarnation and Christian love. He specifically condemns Diotrephes, who aspired to be the local bishop of parishes where John had sent evangelists to investigate reported jurisdictional disputes. Diotrephes had vigorously opposed the evangelists John sent, and lorded over the Church instead of leading it. He was resistant to apostolic oversight and the traditional ways of the Church. Thus John writes to Diotrephes' parish, but he addresses his letter to Gaius because he does not trust Diotrephes. Gaius had fully supported the evangelists whom John had sent. They had highly praised Gaius in their report to John.

19. The Epistle of Jude: Jude, a relative of Jesus (called the "brother" of the Lord in Matthew 13:55 and Matthew 6:3) and the brother of James the Just (Bishop of Jerusalem and author of James), is the author of this epistle. This is *not* the Jude who was one of the twelve and who was called

Thaddaeus or Lebbaeus. The date of this letter is thought to be sometime in the period of 60–80 AD. Time indicators of this letter suggest a maturing first century faith and the letter's themes include the following:

1. The basic doctrines of the faith are seen as fixed and already handed down.
2. The founding expressions of the apostles are described as being in the past (vv.17, 18).
3. Faith is seen as something to be maintained, not discovered (v. 20).

Jude is a treatise directed against false teachers within the Church who are jeopardizing the salvation of many. He supports his attack with examples from the Old Testament, and the necessity of God dealing harshly with those who assault His people. Jude uses 1 Corinthians 10:4, 2 Timothy 3:8, and Revelations as contemporary authorities and takes from them what is pertinent. These books share a similar language and similar purpose as Jude. Many scholars believe that 2 Peter also refers to Jude. James the Just and Jude are associated with Palestine, and Jude makes use of Jewish traditions. But the immorality that Jude attacks is associated more with Gentiles. The heretics whom Jude opposes are present in the Church (vv. 4, 12, 22, 23), carrying on an aggressive campaign of propaganda and subversion. They question authority and are disobedient to the laws that control world order. They ridicule true Christianity and are schismatic and devoid of the Spirit. Jude's purposes, then, are: (a) to rouse the Church to declare war on heresy (v. 3); (b) to exhort the Church to orthodox faith and practice (vv 20, 21); (c) to rescue the weak and fallen where possible (vv. 22, 23); and (d) to instill confidence that God is indeed the Lord of all (vv. 1, 24, 25).

The Bible in the Liturgy

The Word of God present in the holy and divinely inspired scriptures remains the foundation of the Orthodox faith and spirituality. Holy

Scripture is the very substance of the dogmas and liturgies of the Orthodox Church, and through this worship the Church reaches out to its constituents with the Word of God. The Liturgy itself begins with the elevation of the Bible above the altar. In the Small Entrance of the Liturgy, the Bible is carried out before the people and elevated as the priest says, "Wisdom, let us attend." He is telling us to pay special attention, as God is about to share His wisdom with us through this book. This exemplifies an appearance of Christ in our midst today, proclaiming that He continues to speak to us through this book.

As the priest reads the gospel and epistle lesson of the day, Christ continues to be present among us to speak to us through His Word. St. John Chrysostom urges Christians "to read the Sunday gospel lessons at home on Saturday evening and meditate on it." Having the Church Interpretation at hand would give worshipers purpose in the lesson, and application of what Christ is trying to teach us that day. This is how worshipers are to prepare themselves in advance for the reading of the gospel in the Sunday Liturgy. And as they leave Church, their thoughts should linger on how the gospel lessons that were just spoken will strengthen their way of Christian life.

What the Bible Does for Us

The Bible gives us the eternally valid truth of God. It *informs, reforms, and transforms* those who accept it with faith. It *informs* us about Jesus the Son of God, Whom to know is eternal life. It *reforms* us for in it we find the ideal and the standard by which we ought to live. It *transforms* us because in it we are brought face to face with the grace and power of Christ by which all things are made new. We look to other books for information, but we look to the Bible not only for *information*, but also for *reformation* and *transformation*. *It has all three.* Whenever you read the Gospel, Christ Himself is speaking to you. And while you read, you are praying and talking to Him

There have been many recorded instances where reading the Bible and believing in Christ: saved one from a life of crime and drugs; it was a turning point in someone's life; it transformed someone from being a broken, sour, bitter person into a loving, kind, peaceful human being. There are many more occurrences where knowing and loving Jesus Christ was a saving grace in one's life.

Reading the Bible Daily

Orthodox Christians have great respect for the Bible. We kiss it in veneration and honor it in many ways during the Liturgy. But do we honor it in the most important way? Do we open it up to read its treasures? Do we proclaim its glorious good news?

Many Christians claim worn excuses that they don't have time to read the Word of God during the day. But it is really not a question of time as it is to possess a love of Jesus Christ. We always find time for the things we like to do. When we fall in love with the author (Jesus), it will not be a chore to read His personal letter to us. Father Florovsky has written: "No one profits from the gospel unless he is first in love with Christ. For Christ is not a text, but a living Person, and He abides in His body, the Church." The highest form of Bible reading comes to those who have a great love for Jesus, that to read His word is sheer enjoyment and complete satisfaction.

Life is demanding. Our own personal schedule is hectic enough, and many of us not only have the daily demanding routine of jobs, but also that of our children crowded with school and outside activities. Just as Christ withdrew to pray and talk directly to His Father, we should withdraw from our hectic routine a few minutes every day to focus our minds on God. Take the time needed to read the Bible each day.

The Bible is our door to God's kingdom. But a door, unless it is open, is just another part of the wall. How often do we open our door to the kingdom to find God, and to let God find us? The Bible will not become the Word of God for us unless we take it off the shelf and make it a part of our minds and hearts. We should open our hearts and be listening with interest to what God is saying to us through *His Word*. When God speaks, everything He says is directed personally to us. From our standpoint it should become an individual dialogue that touches us personally. Father Peter Chambers, a New Testament scholar, wrote: "Every effort must be made to make our study of the Bible a liturgical experience, a true communion with our Lord and His Holy Spirit."

As a door to God's kingdom, the Bible is to be read *lovingly, expectantly, personally, prayerfully, and faithfully,* allowing the Word of Christ to dwell in us *thoroughly.* It is a prepared book for a prepared people.

Our reading of the Bible is a personal dialogue between each of us and Christ Himself—but we also need guidance. It is necessary to interpret through the Church. If it was the Church that, with the guidance of the Holy Spirit, assembled the books truly representing the Word of Christ, then it is the Church that tells us how Scripture is to be understood. The understanding of what Scripture means is to discover the thought process or "mind of the Church."

A first step in discovering the "mind of the church" is to see how Scripture is used in worship. How are particular biblical lessons chosen for reading on a daily basis during the year? How are they chosen for reading at different feasts and holidays? How do we arrange the scheduling of the readings of the New Testament and the Old Testament? One should strive that on this basis a schedule of readings be planned and implemented for each year. Church Interpretations, similar to those in the Orthodox Study Bible, should also be utilized in our daily readings. The following sources are suggested to establish a schedule for daily Bible readings.

1. Daily Bible Reading Guide for Orthodox Christians* – Prepared by Father William Chiganos; Holy Apostles Greek Orthodox Church; Westchester, Illinois – (708) 562–2744
2. How to Read the New Testament in a Year–The Orthodox Study Bible (13); pp. 781–783
3. The Lectionary: Listings of Bible Readings for all Feast Days and Holidays of the Orthodox Church–The Orthodox Study Bible (13); pp. 771–780
4. Harmony of Events of the New Testament: Lists major events in chronological order; includes the dates of events, related readings in the gospels of Matthew,

Mark, Luke, and John; and related references from the epistles, Revelation, and the Old Testament–The Orthodox Study Bible (13); pp. 838–843

5. The Old Testament–Genesis to Ezra
6. The Old Testament–Nehemiah to Malachi (includes Psalms and Proverbs)

*This includes the listing of the daily Bible readings used by the Church. A complete schedule is composed of a three-year cycle.

It is suggested that the above listings be read in five-year cycles as follows:

First Year – Item #1
Second Year – Item #2
Third Year – Items #3 & #4
Fourth Year – Item #5
Fifth Year – Item #6

Chapter 11
THE FRUIT OF PRAYER

Importance of Prayer

Prayer preceded every major event in the life of Jesus. This illustrates to each of us the importance of prayer in our lives.

When Jesus prayed during His baptism, heaven was opened and the Holy Spirit descended on Him in the form of a dove. Luke 3:21–22 recounts a voice that came from heaven saying, "Thou art my beloved Son; with Thee I am well pleased." Later Jesus prayed the night before choosing His apostles (Luke 6:12–13); He prayed before His transfiguration; He prayed before His crucifixion. By praying and seeking the will of His Father, He displayed complete humility. He trusted His Father because when He did not get His own will, He yielded to God's will. Likewise, we should rely on God through our prayers.

At every great event in Jesus's life He would withdraw into His Father's presence for prayer, and then return to the hectic world to do His Father's will. This set the precedent for two great movements of the *human spirit:* withdrawal into God's presence through prayer for strength and revelation; and return to the world to live life as commanded by our Lord.

God's promises concerning prayer are well described in the Scriptures. "Call to me and I will answer you, and will show you great and hidden things which you have not known" (Jer. 33:3). God's assurances are also described in Matthew 7:7–11: "Ask and it will be given to you; seek and you will find; knock and it will be opened to you. For everyone who asks receives; and he who seeks finds; and to him who knocks it will be opened. Or what man of you, if his son asks him for bread will give him a stone? Or if he asks for a fish, will give him a serpent? If you then, who are evil, know how to give good gifts to your children, how much more will your Father who is in heaven give good things to those who ask him!" *The greatest miracle of all is prayer—for it's our opportunity to speak with our Maker as He speaks to us. The basis of one's spiritual life is church community prayer during the Orthodox Liturgy.*

Most modern industries and businesses normally schedule morning and afternoon coffee breaks, when workers can pause for a few moments and refresh themselves. Efficiency experts have determined that a person will be more productive if given a scheduled break from work. Our spiritual lives share similarities to this. We need "prayer breaks" periodically—special, scheduled times to spend with God in prayer. Such "prayer breaks" make us more poised and productive Christians in our daily walk.

What Is Prayer?

A famous theologian, Theophan, said, "Prayer is to stand with the mind in the heart before God, and to go on standing before Him unceasingly day and night until the end of life." The head seeks God, but it is the heart that finds Him. St. Paul writes, "For man believes in his heart and is so justified" (Romans 10:10). Just as love, charity, and other virtues do not exist only in the mind but are primarily of the heart, so it is with our faith and trust in God. You must pray not only with words, but also with the mind, and the heart must feel what the mind is thinking. All these elements combined together constitute real prayer. If any of them are absent, your prayer then is either imperfect, or no prayer at all. Let the words not remain only on your lips. Let them travel <u>journey</u> from your lips to your mind to your heart.

Father John Krondstadt talks about people who "call prayer that which is not prayer at all: for instance, a man goes to church, stands there for a time, looks at the icons or other people, and says that he has prayed to God; or else he stands before an icon at home, bows his head, says some words that have been learned by heart, without understanding, without feeling, and says that he has prayed—although with his thoughts and his heart he has not prayed at all, but was elsewhere, with other people and other things, and not with God." Prayer is not merely speaking to God with the mind or uttering thoughtless words from the lips. It is descending with the mind into the heart where we can love God, feel His presence, and yield our will to Him.

The mind truly prays by centering its full attention on the words of the prayer. It is also important to envision the specific needs addressed in your prayer. If you are thanking the Lord for the many blessings you have received every day of your life, for all that He has done for you, and for how much He has helped you, then you should envision in your mind specific blessings you have received. If you are thanking Him for the instances that He has helped you—especially in times of crises—and for what He has done for you, envision specifically what you are referring to. If you ask the Lord to forgive your sins and transgressions, then reflect on specific occurrences. These images you should pass on from your mind to your heart and throughout your whole body; then feel the presence of God, and know that He is listening to you. If something is disturbing you, talk it over with God, for He truly cares for you. Tell Him exactly how you feel, for He is your friend. Isaiah says, "Call and the Lord will answer; you shall cry, and He will say, 'Here I am.' Then shall your light rise in the darkness and your gloom be as the noonday."

The Fruit of Prayer

We enjoy a plentiful harvest through the fruit of prayer. A recent study at Harvard revealed that people who pray regularly suffer less from high blood pressure. So one of the fruits of prayer is less pressure, more *inner peace*—because there is more trust in God as the result of praying regularly. I'm sure all of us have heard stories from physicians of patients where even after therapy, chemotherapy, and radiation treatment of cancer the treatments have failed, and yet the fruit of prayer has *healed* the patient with no medical explanation.

Prayer is the only power in the world that seems to overcome the laws of nature. The occasions on which prayer has dramatically done this have been termed miracles.

Just like it did for the apostles on the day of Pentecost, prayer is the key that unlocks the door to the *Holy Spirit* for all of us. It was when they were gathered together in prayer that they were filled with the Holy Spirit. Prayer, as the key that unlocked the door to the Holy Spirit, unites us with God and brings us into His presence. To pray is to be with God; it is a *union with God*.

In addition to the Holy Spirit and union with God, another fruit of prayer is *love*. It comes from our union with God, who Himself is the only source of love. There can be no genuine love unless we are united with the source of love—God. And it is prayer that unites us with God. Young couples who are about to be married should remember that if they desire a strong and lasting relationship in their marriage, they must let God's love flow into their lives through prayer.

The fruit of prayer is inner peace, healing power, the Holy Spirit, union with God, and love. All the sacraments and all the theology of the Church flow from prayer. Its power is tremendous. It unites us with God and truly makes us God-like. It is the ladder to heaven! The whole purpose of the spiritual life is to descend with the mind into the heart through inner prayer and to discover there the kingdom of God. *"The kingdom of God is within you,"* said Jesus (Luke 17:20).

Prayer Guidelines

These suggested guidelines are taken from an Orthodox prayer book. An important part of effective prayer is first having your mind at peace and in a spiritual mode. Use the following guidelines listed below as a starting point for establishing the means to worship so that you might have a continual and permanent bond with the Lord:

1. First try to clear your mind of all thoughts; slowly breathe in and breathe out until you are relaxed. Focus your mind, your senses, and your heart on your prayer.

2. Start your prayer by making the sign of the cross and say aloud: "In the name of the Father, and of the Son, and of the Holy Spirit."

3. Pray to God as if you were having a direct conversation with Him; submit in total to Him your mind, body, and soul with all the force you can generate.

4. Complete your prayer by making the sign of the cross and say aloud: "Holy God, Holy Mighty, Holy Immortal, have mercy on me."

5. During each prayer, thank the Lord for the blessings you receive; ask forgiveness for any sins or transgressions; and include a prayer for loved ones, those who have illnesses, and for any problems you are facing.

Forms of Prayer

When should we pray? How should we pray? How do we express our prayers? These are all questions that we should ask ourselves and find the answers to.

My first experience with prayer was as a child when I noticed my parents saying their prayers every night, and then their morning prayers. Through observing my parents I learned that you start your day with prayers and you end the day in prayer. However, the many prayers that I experienced during the Orthodox Liturgy made me realize that prayers were more than just saying them in the morning and at night. One should also have special prayers when you, for instance, have the feeling that you need God's assistance, or when you want to pray to the Lord for anyone that may be sick or is suffering. When you repeat daily your morning and nightly prayers, recognize your special prayers, descend from the mind into the heart to experience the intimate love of God, then you will find yourself praying on a regular basis and making prayer a natural part of your life. Cultivate daily prayer with God, your Father, and accept the truth that He awaits your every call and will unfailingly respond. If we uphold this practice, we will comprehend that meeting God in prayer is the most important thing we can do each day.

Although prayer is natural, and we were created by God to live a life of prayer, sin has built a barrier between God and us. That is why prayer became fatiguing work after sin entered the world. Whenever we start to pray, Satan and his legions are there to distract us and to try to steal our prayers. To combat this, the Orthodox Church in her great wisdom has given us what is known as the Rule of Prayer. This means that you have to set aside a regular period of time each day and devote it exclusively to prayer. In the following sections, we will describe examples of nightly prayers, morning prayers, and special prayers, in hopes that you will select from them prayers that impact your heart. Allow yourself to embark on a life in which prayer is a normal and regular daily occurrence on a continual basis. *Remember that for each prayer that you say, the specific needs you are praying for should be envisioned and expressed—from your mind to your heart and throughout your whole body. You should get the feeling you are talking directly with God and He is listening to you.*

Nightly Prayers:

Listed below are a number of prayers that can be used as a basis to formulate your nightly prayers. You may be able to expand or add to them.

- Start your prayers by making the sign of the cross and saying: *"Glory to the Father, the Son, and the Holy Spirit."*
- Lord, thank you for the many blessings you have given me every day of my life. You have helped me and done so much for me and you keep blessing me. (At this point, think of the blessings you are thanking Him for—what He has done to help you and what He has done for you.)
- Pray for individuals (names_____) that they may be blessed with the wisdom, commitment, and strength to make the right decisions and stay on the path set out for them; ask that they find peace, love, joy, and happiness throughout their lifetime.

- Pray for those individuals (names_____) who are ill and suffering, that the Lord return them to and keep them in good health, so that they may find peace, joy, love, and happiness throughout their lifetime. *"O Christ, who alone is our defender, visit and heal Your suffering servant(s)_____, delivering them from sickness and grievous pains. Raise them up that they may praise You without ceasing; through the prayers of the Theotokos, You who alone loves mankind."*

- Pray that the divided churches of our Lord Jesus Christ come together as one Church, one Body of Christ; that the one Church, one Body of Christ, make believers of all the people of the world; and that all nations become thrones of God and follow the teachings and instructions of our Lord and Savior; that the nations, as thrones of God, establish a government for the people, of the people, and by the people, and that there be love and harmony among them. May all nations follow the path established by our Lord and work together to eliminate wars, terrorism, poverty, suffering, murders, drugs, crimes, and all evil. That sicknesses, diseases, viruses, and plagues be overcome; that there be peace, love, joy, and harmony among all throughout this world. Thus, we avoid the wrath of God, the final Battle of Armageddon, and the final presence of our Lord here on earth, which would result in total death and destruction; and we here on earth undergo the Second Coming of our Lord Jesus Christ.

- Pray for remission of all your sins and transgressions: *"O Lord our God, if during this day I have sinned, whether in word or deed or thought, forgive me all, for You are good and love mankind."* Ask that He help you to strengthen your weaknesses and overcome your temptations. For you are the first among sinners, and you face the same weaknesses and temptations each day. (At this point, acknowledge and confess to God specific personal sins, weaknesses, and temptations.) Ask that He help you grow stronger spiritually, so you can remain on the path chosen for you, so that you can do His work, help teach His word, and help others to improve the quality of their lives according to His instructions.

- "Pray that you awake tomorrow so that you can glorify God, His Son, and His Holy Spirit." Note: this is actually a prayer directly to God.
- After you have prayed for all your blessings, needs, and requests, repeat the Jesus prayer three times: *"Lord Jesus, Son of God, have mercy on me, a sinner."*
- Closing prayer: *"For to You belong all glory, honor, and praise, Father, Son, and Holy Spirit, now and forever, to the ages of ages. AMEN."*
- End your prayers by making the sign of the cross with: *"Holy God, Holy Mighty, Holy Immortal, have mercy on me."*

More Nightly Prayers:

- Now that the day has ended, I glorify you, O Master, and I pray that I can start a new day, tomorrow, without further sin. Grant this to me, O Savior, and save me.
- Grant me peaceful and undisturbed sleep, and deliver me from the temptations of the evil one.
- Raise me up again in the morning that I may glorify You; for You are blessed with Your only begotten Son and Your all-holy Spirit, now and forevermore. AMEN.
- Lord, thank you for the blessings that you have bestowed on me this day. Grant me to sleep through the night with peace and when I awake provide me the strength and wisdom to continue to live a life of our Lord and Savior, and Your Son, Jesus Christ. Heavenly Father in your love have mercy on your servants (names _____) for whom I pray and commend to your care and protection. Through the mercy of Your Son and Savior Jesus Christ,

and the prayers of his holy Mother, and all the saints. AMEN.

- (Group Prayer) Blessed are You, O God, Almighty Lord, who makes the sun to give light to the day and brightens the night with the shining stars. You have brought us through this long day and led us to the threshold of night. Hear our prayer. Forgive us all the sins we have committed deliberately or in our weakness. For You, indeed, O Lord our God, have mercy on us and save us; and we glorify You, Father, Son, and Holy Spirit, now and forever, to the ages of ages. AMEN.

- (Prayer for the family) And grant rest, O Master, to the souls and bodies of our family as we sleep; preserve us from the dismal slumber of sin and from the dark passions of night. Calm the impulses of sinful desires; quench the fiery darts of the evil one, which are cunningly directed against us. Still the rebellions of the flesh, and put far from us all anxiety and worldly cares.

- Eternal God, King of all creation, who has kept me safe to arrive to this hour, forgive me the sins which I have committed this day in thought, word, and deed. And cleanse, O Lord, my humble soul from every stain of flesh and spirit. Grant me, O Lord, to pass this night in peace, to rise from my bed, and to please Your Holy Name all the days of my life. Deliver me, O Lord, from the vain thoughts that stain me, and from evil desires. For Thine is the Kingdom, and the power, and the glory of the Father, and of the Son, and the Holy Spirit, now and forever, and unto ages of ages. AMEN.

- (Just before going to sleep) Into Your hands, O Lord Jesus Christ, I commend my spirit and body; bless me, save me, and grant me eternal life. AMEN.

- Lord, our God, forgive all the sins I have committed this day in word, deed, and thought, for You are good and love mankind. Grant me a peaceful sleep, free of restlessness. Send Your guardian angel to protect and keep me from all harm. For You are the Guardian of our souls and bodies, and to You we ascribe glory, to the Father, and to the Son, and to the Holy Spirit, now and forevermore. AMEN.

Morning Prayers:

For years I would start and end my morning prayers with the Jesus Prayer. These morning prayers also included various Psalms and prayers that related to how I should start and best utilize my time and efforts that day. The Jesus Prayer, consisting of the simple words, *"Lord Jesus, Son of God, have mercy on me, a sinner,"* is the deepest expression of the spiritual tradition of the Eastern Orthodox Church. It became the center of Orthodox spirituality, not only because of its utmost simplicity, but also in its constant invocation of the all-powerful divine name of Jesus, our Lord and Savior. "There is none other name under heaven given among men, whereby we must be saved" (Acts 10:12). "Wherefore God also has exalted Him, and given Him a Name which is above every name: that at the Name of Jesus every knee should bow, of things in heaven, and things under the earth" (Phil. 2:9–10). In saying the Jesus Prayer, I developed a strong desire to find a way to talk openly to Jesus, to be able to openly converse with Him. Years later I received an e-mail from a lifelong friend of mine that contained a prayer to Jesus, a prayer that she said every day. According to her, this prayer greatly inspired her. I immediately modified the wording to be more consistent with the Orthodox prayers, and in addition I added Psalms and prayers that I had been repeating each morning. The results were astonishing! Each time I repeated the prayer, I got the feeling that I was personally communicating with Jesus Christ. It raised me to another spiritual level. I named it *"The Extended Jesus Prayer."* I offer it to you as a way to regularly personally communicate with our Lord and Savior. As this prayer takes hold in your heart, you will find, as I did, that you will begin to pray unceasingly.

Properly prepare yourself before you read this prayer. Take a moment to relax your mind and humble your heart to focus on

Christ. Allow God to be the only one on your mind while you say this **Extended Jesus Prayer.** We should respectfully talk to Christ with true sincerity and from our deepest inner feelings when we declare this solemn prayer. As you come to each part of the prayer, the specific needs you are praying for should be envisioned and expressed—from your mind to your heart and throughout your whole body. Read this prayer; rather, regularly talk to Jesus through this prayer. Remember to repeat the **Jesus Prayer** before and after you say the **Extended Jesus Prayer** as it is presented below:

THE JESUS PRAYER: *"Lord Jesus, Son of God, have mercy on me, a sinner."*

THE EXTENDED JESUS PRAYER:

Lord Jesus Christ, Son of God, thank You for this day. Thank You for my being able to see and to hear this morning, and for being able to use all the other human attributes I am blessed with. You have done so much for me, and You keep blessing me.

Lord, grant me the willingness to greet the coming day in peace, and help me in all things to rely upon Your holy will. Teach me to treat all that comes to me throughout the day with peace of soul and with firm conviction that Your will governs all. Guide my thoughts and feelings in all my deeds and words. Forgive me this day for everything I will do, say, or think that will not be pleasing to you. Direct my will and teach me to pray for your sanctification.

Please, Our Lord and Savior, keep me safe from all danger and harm. Help me to go through this day with a new attitude and much gratefulness. Let me make the best of each and every day to keep my mind clear so I can hear Your Word, and stay on the path that has been chosen for me. Grant me spiritual growth, faith, and understanding.

Lord, broaden my mind to accept all things and let me not complain and agonize over things of which I have no control. Grant me the serenity to accept the things I cannot change, courage to change the things I can, and wisdom to know the difference.

Have mercy on me, O Lord, according to Your unfailing love; according to your great compassion blot out my transgressions. Help me to strengthen my weaknesses and overcome my temptations. Wash away all my iniquities and cleanse me from my sins.

Let me continue to see sin through God's eyes and acknowledge it as evil. And when I sin, help lead me to repentance, so I can confess through my heart and with my mouth my wrongdoing, and receive the forgiveness of God. I ask now that You, O Lord, have mercy on me, and forgive all my sins and transgressions.

Grant me peace; protect me from all evil and the temptations that I face each day. Awake me each morning that I may glorify Your Father, You, and the Holy Spirit; help me love according to Your will and follow Your commandments. Continue to grant me faith and understanding; help me to grow stronger spiritually and stay on the path chosen for me.

And when this world closes in on me, let me remember, Lord Jesus, Your example, when You would slip away and find a quiet place to pray. It's the best response when I'm pushed beyond my limits. After all, I'm human and not perfect. Only You, Lord, our Savior, are perfect. I know, when I am not in prayer, You will listen to my heart.

Lord Jesus, continue to use me to do Your will. Continue to bless me that I may be a blessing to others. Keep me strong that I may help the weak. Keep me uplifted that I may have words of encouragement for others. Keep me on your path and help me to assist those that are lost and can't find their way. Help us all to continue to have complete faith in you, our Lord.

I pray for all those who are ill and for those less fortunate. I pray for all my sisters and brothers. I pray for peace, love, and joy in their homes and that all their needs are met.

Lord Jesus, help me believe that God changes people and God changes things for the benefit of us all. I pray that every person who reads this prayer knows that there is no problem, or circumstance, or situation that cannot be resolved by the power of God.

Every battle can be won through deep-seated faith in God. O Christ our God, on this day, direct my life according to Your Father's commandments, as taught and exemplified by You, and deliver me from all evil and distress.

O Christ our God, You are worshiped at all times and in all places and are glorified both in heaven and on earth. You are patient, generous in mercy, rich in compassion, loving to the just, and merciful to the sinner. You call all of us to repentance through the promise of blessings to come.

In Jesus's Name, Amen.

THE JESUS PRAYER: "Lord Jesus, Son of God, have mercy on me, a sinner."

Committing to genuinely use the ***Extended Jesus Prayer*** on a regular basis will bring you to a degree where you feel you are walking side by side with our Lord and Savior Jesus Christ, the Son of God.

More Morning Prayers:
- Lord our God, teach me Your righteousness and Your wisdom. Enlighten my mind that I not reside in the sin that leads to death of the soul. Let me greet the new day with gladness and offer you my morning prayer. For Yours is the greatness, the majesty, the power, and the glory, Father, Son, and Holy Spirit, now and forever, to the ages of ages. AMEN.
- O Lord, grant me the strength to endure the weariness of the coming day and all the events that take place. Direct my will and teach me to pray, to believe, to hope, to be patient, to forgive, and to love. AMEN.

- In rising from sleep to begin another day, O Holy Trinity—Father, Son, and Holy Spirit—I give thanks to You for being so patient with me in Your great goodness, for never showing any anger with me in spite of my failings and laziness, and for refusing to let me suffer in my sins. Instead, You have shown me Your great love for mankind over and over again, raising me up from every new trouble I fall into again and again. Enlighten the eyes of my mind and heart, and open my lips to ponder and reflect on Your Word, to come to an understanding of Your commandments; to do Your will in all things; and to sing to You from the depths of my heart, forever glorifying your most holy name, Father, Son, and Holy Spirit; now and forever. AMEN.
- O Lord, I give You wholehearted thanks for the gift of a new day, with its opportunities of pleasing You. Grant that I may so pass its hours in the perfect freedom of Your service. At every event, may I again give thanks to You; through Jesus Christ our Lord. AMEN.
- O Lord grant me the wisdom, strength and courage to meet the coming say in peace. Help me to do your will and carry out this day in love and harmony. I thank you for your great goodness and patience. Enlighten my mind and open my ears to hear your words and commandments and to praise your all-holy Name Father, Son and Holy Spirit, now and forever. AMEN
- Arising from sleep, I thank You, O Most Holy Trinity, for the sake of Your great kindness and understanding. You have not had resentment against me, for I am apathetic and sinful. Neither have You shattered me in my transgressions. But You have shown me your customary love toward mankind, that I might sing my morning praise to You and glorify Your power. Enlighten my eyes of my acceptance, open my ears to receive Your words, and teach me Your commandments. Help me to do Your will, to sing Your praises, to confess to You

from my heart, and to praise Your all-holy name: of the Father, and of the Son, and of the Holy Spirit, now and forever, and unto the ages. AMEN.

Special Prayers:

There may be events, including personal, family, or group events, that may involve special prayers related to a specific occasion. One can more greatly emphasize the special prayers by including a holy prayer, such as the Orthodox *Trisagion Prayer*, shown below. Saying it before and/or after the special prayer puts more meaning into the specific events for which you wish to pray.

Trisagion Prayer:
In the name of the Father and of the Son and of the Holy Spirit. Amen. Glory to You, our God, Glory to You.

O Heavenly King, the Comforter, the Spirit of Truth: You are everywhere satisfying all things. Treasury of blessings and Giver of Life: come and abide in us, and cleanse us from every iniquity, and save our souls. O Good One!

Holy God! Holy Mighty! Holy Immortal! Have mercy on us. (Repeat 3 times.)
Glory to the Father and to the Son and to the Holy Spirit, now and ever unto the ages. Amen.

O Most Holy Trinity, have mercy on us!
O Lord, cleanse us from our sins!
O Master, pardon our transgressions!
O Holy One, visit and heal our infirmities for Your name's sake.

Lord have mercy. (Repeat 3 times.)
Glory to the Father and to the Son and to the Holy Spirit, now and forever and unto ages of ages. Amen.

End with the Lord's Prayer

From Psalm 51—King David's Confession:
Have mercy on me, O God according to Your unfailing love; according to Your great compassion blot out my transgressions. Wash away all my iniquities and cleanse me from my sin. For I know my transgressions, and my sin is always before me. Create in me a pure heart, O God, and renew a steadfast spirit within me. Do not cast me from your presence, or take your Holy Spirit from me. Restore to me the joy of your salvation and grant me a willing spirit to sustain me. Then I will teach transgressors Your ways, and sinners shall turn back to you. AMEN.

Prayer for Forgiveness – Lord, God our Father, if during this day I have sinned in word, deed or thought forgive me in your goodness and love. Grant me peace; protect me from all evil and the temptations that I continue to face throughout the day. Awake me each morning that I may glorify You, Your Son and Your Holy Spirit now and forever and ever. AMEN.

Family Prayer to Receive the Holy Spirit:
O God, You have graciously brought us to this hour. Just as You poured out Your Holy Spirit upon Your apostles, filling them with the gift of your grace, so, most wonderful Lord, may we too receive this blessing; and as we seek to praise You, merciful God, may we share in Your eternal Kingdom. For Your name is worthy of all honor and majesty; Father, Son, and Holy Spirit, now and forever, to the ages of ages. AMEN.

Prayer Before Meals:
In the name of the Father, and of the Son, and of the Holy Spirit. AMEN.

Say the Lord's Prayer.

Glory to the Father, and to the Son, and to the Holy Spirit, now and forever and unto the ages of ages. AMEN.

Lord have mercy. (Repeat 3 times.)

Christ our God, bless us Your servants and the food and drink that we have before us. You are holy always, now and forever and to the ages of ages. AMEN.

Prayer Before Meals:
Lord, Jesus Christ, Son of God, bless us your servants, this food and drink that we have before us, for You O Lord are the Source of all blessings, now and forever and ever. AMEN

Prayer After Meals:
Blessed is God, who has mercy on us and nourishes us from His bountiful gifts by His grace and compassion always now and forever and unto the ages of ages. AMEN.

Prayer to God:

Let Your mercy be upon me, O Lord, even as I have set my hope on You. Blessed are You, O Lord; teach me Your statutes
Blessed are You, O Master; make me understand Your commandments.
Blessed are You, O Holy One; enlighten me with Your precepts.
Your mercy endures forever, O Lord! To You belongs worship, to You belongs praise, to You belongs glory. To the Father and to the Son and to the Holy Spirit, now and forever and unto ages of ages. AMEN.

Prayer to Christ

O Christ our God, who at all times and in every hour in heaven and on earth is worshiped and glorified; you who is longsuffering, merciful, and compassionate; who loves the just and shows mercy upon sinners; who calls all to salvation through the promise of the good things to come. O Lord, in this hour receive my supplications and direct my life according to Your commandments. Sanctify my soul, purify my body, correct my thoughts, cleanse my mind; deliver me from all tribulation, evil, and distress. Surround me with Your holy angels, so that guided and guarded by them I can attain to the unity of the faith and to the full knowledge of Your unapproachable glory. For You are blessed unto the ages. AMEN.

Prayer to the Holy Spirit

O Heavenly King, Comforter, the Spirit of Truth, present in all places and filling all Things, treasury of good things and giver of life, come and dwell in me and purify me from every stain, and of Your goodness save my soul.

Prayer to the Theotokos:

O exceedingly glorious and ever-virgin Theotokos, bring my petitions before your Son, and our God, and implore Him that through you He will grant my wishes and save my soul.

Prayer for the Sick:

O Christ, who alone is our defender, visit and heal Your suffering servant(s) (names_____), delivering them from sickness and grievous pains. Raise them up that they may sing to You and praise You without ceasing; through the prayers of the Theotokos, O You, who alone loves mankind.

Prayer for Forgiveness:

Lord, God our Father, if during the day I have sinned in word, deed, or thought, forgive me in your goodness and love. Grant me peace; protect me from all evil and the temptations that I continue to face throughout the day. Awake me each morning that I may glorify You, Your Son, and your Holy Spirit; now and forever. AMEN.

Lenten Prayer of St. Ephraim (kneel during prayer):

Lord and Master of my life, deliver me from the spirit of laziness, meddling, ambition, and gossip. Give me, Your servant, the spirit of prudence, humility, patience, and love. Lord and King, grant that I may see sins and faults and not judge my brothers and sisters, for You are blessed forever and ever. AMEN

A Prayer before Undertaking Any Task:

Almighty God, our help and refuge, source of all wisdom and pillar of strength. You know that without You I am powerless. I firmly believe that apart from You I can do nothing. Send Your grace to enable me to complete the task I am about to undertake. Help me to accomplish it faithfully and diligently so that it may prove helpful to myself and others, and that it may bring glory to Your holy name. For Yours is the kingdom and the power and the glory of the Father and the Son and the Holy Spirit now and forevermore. AMEN.

Prayer for the Dead:

Along with Your saints, O Christ, give rest to the soul of Your servant (name_____), in a place where there is neither pain, nor grief, nor longing, but life everlasting. AMEN.

Prayer for One Who Is Dying

Receive in peace the soul of Your servant (name_____), and give him rest in Your eternal dwelling with all Your saints, by the grace of Your only Son our Lord and God and Savior, Jesus Christ, with whom You are blessed together with Your all-holy, gracious, and life-giving Spirit, now and forever and unto ages of ages. AMEN.

Commemoration for the Departed:

Remember, O Lord, the souls of Your servants now fallen asleep; our fathers, mothers, brothers, sisters, children, and friends; all our loved ones and all Christians throughout the world. Forgive them all their sins, committed knowingly or unknowingly; grant them your kingdom, a portion in Your eternal blessing, and the enjoyment of Your unending life. AMEN

Chapter 12
GOD IS WITH US AND ALL AROUND US

There is what is thought to be common rationale among many scientists that God is in no way linked to pure science. This assumption that God and science are distinct and separated can't be further from the truth! An evaluation of the order of atoms and similar order in the universe, the human body, conception and births, and all phases of science shows that there is some greater power who created and established all these highly organized processes. They are methodically structured and function in such a consistent manner that can only be explained by an intelligent designer, a creator who is infinite and absolute in power. "When I consider your heavens, the work of your fingers, the moon and the stars, which you have set in place, what is man that you are mindful of him, and the son of man that you care for him? You made him a little lower than the angels and crowned him with glory and honor. You made him to have dominion over the works of your hands; you put everything under his feet: all flocks and herds, and the beasts of the field, the birds of the air, and the fish of the sea that pass through the paths of the seas" (Psalm of David 8:3–8).

All we have to do is look all around us to see evidence of God's hand. The natural order of our planet earth in the universe; human life; animal life; plant life; everyday rotation of day and night; the four seasons over a standard year; the sun maintaining the proper global temperatures to permit a balance of the earth's surface and for all life to exist throughout; and the earth's atmospheric composition consisting of the proper proportions of oxygen, nitrogen, and other gases so that all life is sustained on earth. Were these all perfectly aligned circumstances established by random chance? Not at all! All these, among the countless other natural illustrations, are part of a plan that is beyond our total comprehension.

The order of the universe and the planet earth is unimaginable in how it was formed, and how it has been sustained in a systematic fashion for millions of years. Earth is surrounded with a proper atmosphere at the appropriate levels and composition that can sustain human, animal, and plant life. Forces of gravity have been put in place in such a manner as to allow humans, animals, and other objects to remain on the earth's terrestrial and aquatic surfaces, rather than floating out of control away from the earth's exterior. A process is in place to uphold life on earth through the emergence of new generations of humans, animals, and plants. Also, life is sustained of various species under the oceans, seas, and rivers of the earth. All of these minute details attest to God's planned design of a functioning and thriving planet.

WONDERS OF GOD'S CREATION

Human Life

One of the most brilliant and outstanding achievements of our Creator is the design and formation of the human body. "So God created man in His own image, in the image of God He created him; male and female He created them. God blessed them and said to them, 'Be fruitful and increase in number; fill the earth and subdue it'" (Genesis 1:27, 28). God created human life as the crown of His creation! The brilliance and marvels of the function of the human body—tasks like vision, touch, thought process, memory, emotion, responses, and movements of the various parts of the body—work so well, yet we go about our lives and seldom give a second thought to the perfection and the physical and mental wonders of our own human makeup. Deep down we do realize, however, that the human body is the highest expression of our Creator's power.

It's hard to comprehend the mystery of how such a complicated and amazing human form can be established and developed with such outstanding physical and mental characteristics. The process is initiated when a male sperm joins with a female egg to form a cell called an embryo, which develops into a human body in a set period of nine months. The initial cell embryo begins to divide into other cells after thirty hours from the formation of the embryo; this begins the formation of the various parts of the human form. The brain and heart form soon after, and the heart self-starts and begins to beat after two weeks. The organs then appear and develop. The human form of the child starts to take shape after eight weeks when it is only one inch in height. This process continues until the birth of the baby, at which time seeing the baby makes us realize that we are seeing the highest manifestation of God's creative power. A human body with two arms and two legs; ten fingers and ten toes in the same consistent form; two eyes, which are apparent in creating sight for the baby; and a voice which is evident in the form of crying. A heart circulates the blood through thousands of blood vessels throughout the body to support life and helps maintain stable body conditions.

The miracle of childbirth is obvious from the reaction of the parents and others present at birth of a human creation when the baby is first observed. The sudden, deep, unlimited, and permanent love for the newborn demonstrated by the parents is indescribable. A Psalm of David reminds us, "You created my inmost being."

After birth the activity of the cells are regulated with astonishing balance and purpose. Tendons, kneecaps, and surrounding muscles develop. From birth to maturity the cells are replaced at least once each year and the outer layer of skin is replaced every two to four weeks.

The human skeletal system, which consists of 206 bones, is linked together with cartilage and tissue, and is regenerated every twelve months until maturity is reached. Parts of the skeleton are coated with a remarkable lubricant system and are made to move by way of joints. Tendons drive the fingers. The hand with the fingers and thumb can create fifty-eight different movements.

The creation of the brain and how it systematically operates physical, emotional, and other senses—which keep the body working in an orderly manner—is beyond our understanding. The brain is a mass of tissue the size of a three-pound cantaloupe. It operates the thought and memory process and gives us the capacity to speak in the top layer or cortex; the feelings and emotions in the second layer; and the human functions—breathing, movement, etc.—in the third layer. It is in itself beyond comprehension how it is initiated, established, and formulated to achieve the intellectual capacity of the human process. Millions of tiny nerve cells, called neurons, interpret 100 million signals per second. Only selected signals are responded to, and the irrelevant ones are shut out. Not only is it difficult to envision how such an operation proceeds to establish the human body functions, but also it has never been determined as to what initiates it in the human fetus and gets it to advance to its optimum form. What process is present to allow us to individually generate a specific thought or incentive to motivate us to a desired action has never been defined.

Through education and experience we continue to learn throughout life—to learn to speak; how to operate our physical attributes; and how to control our thought processes with proper responses. The brain is the greatest computer that can be assembled. It only requires automatic or planned feedback, or input from the individual, to achieve a result. It is far too complicated for humans to comprehend, assemble, assimilate, and completely replicate in our own man-made computers.

The beating heart is a mechanism of spectacular performance pumping 1800 gallons per day of blood throughout the human body, which turns out to be 50 million gallons in a lifetime. It weighs less than one pound and is the size of a human hand. The heart beats 100,000 times per day, which transcends into 2 billion times over an average life span. This self-starting pump runs without any fuel or power to enable the more than 500 billion red blood cells in a human body to flow through millions of miles of pipeline to provide the oxygen, nutrients, and water necessary to sustain life. Electrical discharges emerge from each cell and are synchronized from one cell to the other. The heart requires no feedback, power, or force to continue to operate. Only life's sustaining power.

In chemical makeup we resemble the dust of the earth, but the formation and organization of the human body results in being creative to fulfill a life full of hopes and dreams and bringing them to reality. We see wonders performed every day by scientists; athletes; in medicine, where doctors perform body surgery, organ replacements, and medical advances; among others. One of the greatest examples of human wonders in our history is the musical composer, Ludwig Von Beethoven, who composed seven of his nine symphonies and dozens of his concerts after he became deaf. These are all examples of mortal man meeting eternal God in meaningful fellowship so that the crowning act of all creation is complete. "Praise the Lord, O my soul; all my inmost being, praise His Holy Name. Praise the Lord, O my soul, and forget not all His benefits—Who redeems your life from destruction and crowns you with love and compassion" (Psalm of David 103:1, 2, 4).

The Planet Earth

One of the greatest astronomical scientists in our history, Verner Von Braun, once said: "One cannot be exposed to the law and order of the universe without concluding that there must be design and purpose to it all." As you look up to a universe where the stars outnumber the grains of sand on all the ocean shores, the wonder of God's work will shine, not only through the infinite cosmos that fills your eyes, but from the very creation where one stands—planet earth. A Psalm of David proclaims, "How many are thy works O Lord..." The more we learn about our solar system, the more unique our earth appears to us. The more we study about our universe, the more we come to realize that the most ideal place suited for life in our entire solar system, and perhaps the entire universe, is the planet we call home.

There are an abundant number of chemical treasures found within our planet earth. The first is the water of life—truly a liquid treasure. More than 60 percent of every human body consists of water (2 hydrogen + 1 oxygen). It is a universal solvent that dissolves many solids without expanding in volume. It is an agent of collection and supply of nutrients and other chemicals necessary for human, animal, and plant life. It is vital and essential to life on earth. The Lord sustains the earth and the life on it by providing the water necessary through rainstorms, thunderstorms, and snowstorms.

The salty oceans make up 97 percent of the water on earth. The water is purified for the earth's requirements through the heat of the sun by vaporizing into the atmosphere in the form of clouds. Storms regenerate the fresh water supply needed on earth. A typical storm releases more power than a 100-Kiloton nuclear bomb. (Note: the explosion of a 1-Kiloton bomb in the center of a crowded city would destroy more than 100,000 people.) Since earth's creation, water on earth has neither significantly increased nor diminished in overall total volume.

There are 96 known basic atomic chemical elements which combine based on known chemical and physical principles to form all chemical matter here on earth. This includes the human body and all of its parts. Natural formations of chemicals provide the human and animal kingdoms with what's needed to sustain life. Man has used the chemical and physical principles to develop and produce the chemical materials that supplement the needs of human life.

The Creator's formula for life on earth involves a multitude of factors and ingredients all working together in precise balance. Isaiah, the Old Testament prophet, said, "He is the God Who formed the earth and made it. He established it and did not create a place of waste, but formed it to be inhabited." The equatorial diameter of the earth is 7927 miles. The planet earth has a rate of rotation of 360 degrees every 23 hours, 56 min., 4 sec.; and an orbital duration of 365 days, 5 hours, 48 min., 45 sec. The atmosphere's composition of 78% nitrogen, 21% oxygen, and 1% of other gases sustains life and surrounds the earth with a required depth to act as a protective layer against the sun—which is at a distance of 93 million miles from the earth. This results in an average temperature of 59 degrees Fahrenheit for the earth's surface. As comparison, Venus, which is about the same size as earth, is 67 million miles from the sun and has an average surface temperature of 900 degrees Fahrenheit, which is hot enough to melt copper. Certainly it is too hot to sustain life.

The fingerprints of God are indelibly etched through the beasts of the earth, the birds of the air, the fish of the sea, and all the remaining animal kingdom. More than 700,000 diverse animal species—mammals, insects, reptiles, birds, marine life, and so on—inherit the earth. Each is designed by God to survive the challenges and demands of everyday existence. Each animal has a unique and specific means of finding and consuming food in order to survive, and many of the animals are sources of food for humans.

The plant kingdom on earth consists of 300,000 different species of plants. These not only add to the beauty of our planet, but also are sources of food, clothing, and shelter. Medicines are derived from their stalks and roots. Most of the oxygen we breathe is released from their leaves. The natural order set up by God for the inherent dispersion of seeds from each plant to the ground assures the continuity of plant life in our world.

God not only created a place we could live in, but one we could enjoy—equipped with beautiful forests; high snow-topped mountains; painted deserts; spacious and well-patterned canyons; green pastures; and breathtaking beauty. "Now the Lord God had planted a garden in Eden; and there He put the man He had formed. And the Lord God made all kinds of trees grow out of the ground—trees that were pleasing to the eye and good for food. A river watering the garden flowed from Eden; from there it was separated into four headwaters—the Pishon; the Gihon; the Tigris, and the Euphrates (Gen. 2:8–14)."

As inhabitants of the earth, we are passengers of a unique and remarkable spacecraft. There is an abundance of flowing water; a favorable planet pattern; fertile soil; life-supporting atmosphere; ideal size and gravitational pull; surrounded by a protective magnetic field; and optimum location in the solar system. The earth couldn't have been designed more perfectly.

Is There Truly Proof and Substantiation?

The discussions above confirm the existence of a Creator who was responsible for our presence here on a planet that provides for life and the continuity of its existence. Everything is arranged in an orderly and organized manner, and there is a grand purpose in every aspect of the human, animal, and plant kingdoms—and the planet earth within an infinite universe. The evidence found in nature and in science truly confirms that *God is all around us and with us*. But what you see is just the tip of the iceberg. If all the aspects and support for intelligent design were included, it would fill an endless number of volumes of books. Ultimately, God designed the earth with purpose, just as He designed you with purpose: to glorify Him.

REFERENCES

1. *The Orthodox Church, A Well-Kept Secret – A Journey Through Church History*, Father George Nicozin

2. *History of The Orthodox Church*, Reverend Constantine Callinikos, B.D.

3. *Introducing The Orthodox Church*, Father Anthony Coniaris

4. *The Orthodox Church*, Timothy Ware

5. *The Orthodox Way*, Bishop Kallistos (Timothy Ware)

6. *The Eastern Orthodox Church – It's Thought and Life*, Ernst Benz

7. *Becoming Orthodox*, Peter Gilchrist

8. *Orthodox Worship*, Williams & Anstall

9. *Living The Liturgy*, Stanley S. Harakas

10. *Contemporary Moral Issues*, Father Stanley Harakas

11. *A Companion To The Orthodox Church*, Edited by Dr. Fotios Litsas

12. *All That A Greek Orthodox Should Know*, Rev. Nicon Patrinacos

13. *Discovering The Rich Heritage of Orthodoxy*, Father Charles Bell

14. *My Daily Orthodox Prayer Book* – Compiled by Anthony M. Coniaris

15. *The Orthodox Study Bible – Discovering Orthodox Christianity in the Pages of The New Testament and The Psalms – New King James Version*, St. Athanasius Orthodox Academy

16. *The Holy Bible – New International Version*, International Bible Society

17. *The Divine Liturgy of St. John Chrysostom and Hymnal* – Translated and Compiled by the Rev. Alexander G. Leondis; Rev. Socrates C. Tsamutalis; and Rev. James C. Moulketis

18. *The Wonders of God's Creation; Videotapes by* Moody Institute of Science, Chicago, IL.